# Kestrels for Company

GORDON RIDDLE

Whittles Publishing

To my parents, who started me off with *The Observer's Book of Birds* and then the *Peterson Field Guide* and my family without whose support this book would not have been written. For my grand-daughters Kate and Emma who I know will grow up enjoying the wildlife around them.

Published by
**Whittles Publishing Ltd.,**
Dunbeath,
Caithness, KW6 6EG,
Scotland, UK

**www.whittlespublishing.com**

ISBN 978-184995-029-9

Printed by

# Contents

# *Foreword*

As a schoolboy in Ayrshire in the early 1970s, like most of my peers, I had a great love of the outdoors and a relatively sound knowledge of the different birds that were to be found in that part of the world. Things were very different then, of course, with no computers, play stations, mobile phones or myriad other options open to many youngsters nowadays in spending their free time. Long days and evenings raking about in the countryside were the norm for us back then, yet most adults seemed to gravitate indoors whenever they could.

Imagine my surprise, then, when I learned of a grown man from Culzean who spent his spare time working on kestrels, and who indeed was a respected expert on the species! Not only that, but teachers put word around my school that any sightings of breeding kestrels were to be reported in order that Mr Riddle could in turn be informed. Somehow, here was a man who had retained that youthful fascination for birds and who so loved the kestrel that he spent much of his time studying them. Almost 40 years later, Gordon's admiration and enthusiasm for this wonderful bird are undiminished, and he has developed an encyclopaedic knowledge of their biology and behaviour that can only come from decades of detailed field observation and recording. A founding member of the south-west Scotland raptor study movement, he has been chairman of the south Strathclyde group for 27 years and in 2010 received the Donald & Jeff Watson Raptor Award from the Scottish Raptor Study Groups.

Gordon modestly insists it's easy to love the kestrel, perhaps the most instantly recognisable and widespread bird of prey in the UK, with its warm plumage and distinctive, at times almost miraculous, hovering action. Active from the first rays of dawn to the dying embers of dusk, this nomadic and somewhat enigmatic raptor makes a remarkable case study. In *Seasons with the Kestrel* we read about the detailed study of breeding kestrels in south Ayrshire and neighbouring areas of Dumfries & Galloway. In *Kestrels for Company*, Gordon now takes his work to a new level. In addition to the intimate study and description of the kestrel's lifestyle and breeding success, we are given intriguing and entertaining anecdotes, including colourful accounts of visits overseas to see Seychelles and Mauritius kestrels.

Moreover, this book contains an informative account of the kestrel's place in the British countryside and how its numbers have fluctuated over the years. This story, remarkable enough in itself, is given context by an examination of the changes in status, acceptance and promotion of other raptors, including conservation measures, reintroductions and important comment on the human pressures that still blight the fortunes of these wonderful birds (or this wonderful group?). This book is therefore a significant addition to raptor study, lovingly written by a dedicated and expert fieldworker, who has been heavily involved with their conservation for almost 40 years.

Chris Rollie, RSPB Scotland Area Manager for Dumfries & Galloway

# Preface

My book *Seasons with the Kestrel* was published nearly 20 years ago and much has happened since then. The raptor map of Britain has changed dramatically, with the recovery of many species from the lows of the pesticide period. There have been changes in land use, such as a reduction in first- rotation commercial forestry planting and agricultural intensification, while pressure from a much more environmentally-aware general public, the diversification of the rural economy by eco-tourism and the work of conservation organisations like the RSPB have generated the political will to improve the protective legislation for our birds of prey.

Their populations, though, are still not at the level which our countryside could support. Things have undoubtedly improved but we have still not rid ourselves of an anti-raptor culture which has no place in the modern age, and the resultant persecution which does so much harm both to our native raptors and to our conservation reputation. The poisoning of raptors is still a blight on our countryside.

The kestrel has not been immune to change and in many areas of Britain it has, in fact, declined. Using as a basis the fieldwork results from my long-term Ayrshire study, which now spans 39 consecutive seasons, and pulling in as much data as possible from other sources, I have tried to put the kestrel's status in perspective. A Scottish slant is inevitable and I do not apologise for it. I hope that this book will maintain the kestrel's profile, encouraging more people to engage with this superb little falcon and to contribute towards its conservation. Much more work is needed to evaluate the current decline and to take the necessary steps to ensure that it remains a key part of our fauna.

# Acknowledgements

Many individuals, groups and organisations have been invaluable in supporting both my kestrel work and the writing of this book and I would like to thank them most sincerely. My son, Keith Riddle, Mike Blair, Karen Gardiner, Fred Westcote and Deirdre Mackinnon provided invaluable IT and photographic assistance; members of the South Strathclyde and Dumfries and Galloway Raptor Study Groups supplied vital data, in particular Ricky Gladwell, Charlie Park, Geoff Shaw, Geoff Sheppard, Gibby McWhirter, Ian Todd, Angus Hogg, Ged Connolly, Bob Stakim, David Gray and Jim Thomson.

Access and co-operation were forthcoming from the British Trust for Ornithology, the Royal Society for the Protection of Birds, Scottish Natural Heritage, the National Trust for Scotland, Scottish Water, Forestry Commission, Natural Research, Scottish Power and the Scottish Ornithologists' Club. Thanks are also due to the people in the study areas who welcomed me on their ground – Nick and Kirstin Parry, James Murdoch, the McWhirter family, the Campbells, Culzean and Cassillis Estates and David Macmillan.

The list of individuals is long and I apologise to anyone whom I have inadvertently missed: Duncan Cameron, Brian Etheridge, Eric Meek, Brian Little, George Morrison, Kevin Duffy, Carl Jones, David Bird, the late John Collie, the late Dick Roxburgh, the late Donald Watson, the late David Shearlaw, Tom Cameron, Paul Hayworth, Dave Dick, Vivien and the late Douglas Bremner, Bob Swann, Jen Smart, Ruth Tingay, Bob McMillan, Dave Anderson, Mick Marquiss, David Jardine, Malcolm Henderson, Bill Wiseman, Keith Miller, Andy Thorpe, Arjun Amar, Steve Petty, Norman Elkins, John Lusby, Victor Colhoun for his joinery expertise in building nest boxes and Kees Hazevoet, Pedrin and Juliao for their assistance on the Cape Verde Islands.

Special mention must be given to Chris Rollie and Deirdre Mackinnon for proof-reading chapters, to Deirdre for her fieldwork backup, to my daughter, Gael Riddle, who assisted with fieldwork and readily climbed trees, and finally to my wife Rosemary, whose support and work on the book has been phenomenal.

Harry Tempest for the barn owl and kestrel in the same nest, Richard Clarkson for the albino hen harrier chick, Chris Rollie for the three grand old men of Galloway, Kevin Simmons for the tern at the pipe, Damian Waters for the barn owl being mobbed by kestrels, Kestrel Press for the logo, Derek Burleigh for the nest site in Majorca, Dave Dick for the cage trap, the late Jeff Watson for the Seychelles kestrel with young at the nest, the late John Collie for the kestrel on the washing line, Martin Carty for White 4 and the reintroduction group, Dave Anderson for the goshawk, Lorcan O'Toole for Red H in flight, Kevin Duffy for the windfarm casualties, Andy Thorpe for the oil rig material, Dave Walker for the young kestrel preyed upon by the golden eagle, RSPB Scotland for the dead eagle, Ewan Greenwood for the cartoon, Scott Smith for male kestrel on the post in the last chapter, Deirdre Mackinnon and Rosemary Riddle for photographs of the author. The remainder are from the author's collection.

# 1

# *An all-consuming passion*

The beginning of each kestrel breeding season comes with certain guarantees. I know that I will at times be very wet and very tired, while blank days and bouts of frustration will be balanced by elation and surprises. There will be special moments. Blood – invariably mine – will be shed. Each season does, though, start with a clean slate: no two are the same and each is a fresh challenge. The target is to have done enough fieldwork by the end of July to give an accurate assessment of the breeding season and be able to put it in the context of previous years.

When people ask me what I do in my spare time, my reply that I study the kestrel is often greeted with a blank look. That's understandable, given that relatively few people choose to devote a great deal of time to climbing trees, being chewed by midges, torn by talons and verbally abused by birds of prey. What has become routine to me is not, I realise, everyone's idea of a recreational pursuit.

Take, for example, one of my last evening outings at the end of July 2000. It had been a very long season and one pair, which had failed early on, had laid a second clutch of eggs. All the other broods had been ringed and had fledged before I'd taken a short break on the Isle of

*Male kestrel in typical roadside perch-hunting mode*

Canna. On the drive to the wood I wondered if the young had survived, because late breeders are not usually very successful.

It was a beautiful, calm, sunny evening, typical of the year as the west of Scotland had avoided the monsoon weather which had plagued the rest of Britain in the new millennium. I sat in the car for a few minutes, scanning the wood for any sign of the adult kestrels, but nothing stirred. This approach is standard practice, allowing time to take in the scene and absorb every available piece of information which could be of use.

Before heading for the nest site, I checked a second nest box at the top of the wood for the barn owl which had taken up residence only that season. Sure enough, there she was, still tucked in at the side of the open-fronted box, not yet ready for her evening foray.

The well-worn path through the unbrashed spruce had long since ceased to pose problems, with most of the lower branches now either pulled back or snapped off. Standing at the foot of a fine sitka spruce, I could see that the box, ten metres above in the canopy, was liberally whitewashed with droppings, as were the branches below. That was reassuring but not 100% proof of success. The young had to be well advanced by that stage and the ringing process would be a delicate operation, with a mass exodus from the nest a distinct possibility.

I thought that the best bet was to carry out the ringing up the tree, so I climbed with all the gear in my shoulder bag. By this time in the season the climb was effortless, but I slowly edged round the back of the box, trying not to precipitate an explosion of startled birds. Peering through the crack in the side of the box, my fears were realized: five well-feathered brown chicks, alert and ready for the off.

The best strategy was simply to take off my jacket and drape it ever so slowly over the front of the box, which I managed to do without a flicker of reaction from the birds. So far, so good. I then took the ringing gear out of the bag and carefully laid the rings on top of the box, the pliers tied round my right wrist (which was also in charge of keeping me balanced) and the bag open, ready to receive the first statistic.

The next stage was the most painful, as I slowly pushed one hand past the coat and into the box and tried to catch one of the birds. This was done completely blind, but there was enough light percolating through the gap to give the birds a clear target. There was no way to avoid the pain as the talons raked my hand, but I did at least get the chance to grab the birds' bodies one by one, pulling them from the box to be ringed and popped into the bag. These birds were ready to fly: not a scrap of down between them and their flight and tail feathers fully developed.

Once all five had been ringed, I returned them one by one to the box as carefully as I had taken them out and slowly removed the jacket. Thankfully, all five young stayed in the box. The whole operation had taken around 20 minutes without a cheep from the adults, which must have been away hunting. If they had been anywhere nearby, they would surely have reacted to the young calling as they were removed from the box.

That one visit sums up most of what I get from working with kestrels – close contact with wild birds, fresh air and physical exercise and the satisfaction of collecting valuable information without adversely affecting the welfare of the birds. It's a physical relationship for six months of the year and a paper one for the rest.

There is always an element of risk in this type of work and safety, of course, is an issue. If I carry out fieldwork on my own, I leave details of my route at home and have taken to carrying a mobile phone. Experience and common sense get me through most things, but, that said, I

*Cliff face layout showing nest locations*

certainly broke the rules on another occasion in the 2000 season. With a brood very close to fledging, I took a chance and was lucky to get away with it.

Gibby McWhirter, one of my contacts and a member of the local Raptor Study Group, had been keeping an eye on a breeding pair in a coastal quarry which had a history of both raven and kestrel occupation. He telephoned to say that the young birds were quite large and that he could see them sitting at the edge of the nest site, an old jackdaw hole in the ivy.

We set off with a ladder on a dry night. On reaching the site and checking through the binoculars, it was clear that the birds were on the point of flying. The commitment to getting the data becomes exceedingly strong and in this case overrode common sense. We carried the ladder to the bottom of the cliff face, hauled it up to a reasonable ledge and made our way gingerly along until we were directly below the site. It was only at this point that we realized that the ledge on which we were to position the ladder was not only narrow, but also sloped ever so gently downwards away from the cliff.

Undaunted, and with the adrenalin pumping, Gibby stood with his back to the cliff and held the ladder out in front of him while I swung out almost into fresh air. I climbed until I was eyeballing three large, brown and distinctly unhappy kestrels. Distinctly unhappy, just like us. The ladder was perched on the very edge of the ledge and I had been forced to climb on from the side.

I managed to grab one bird while holding, white-knuckled, onto the ladder. As soon as I started to climb down, though, the remaining birds burst from the nest and flew with some authority onto the grassy hillside opposite. Both Gibby and I automatically pinpointed the landing places. Bagging, ringing and returning the young bird to the nest site took no time at all and we retreated as quickly as the narrow ledges would permit. It was a fairly simple task to capture and ring the second escapee, which had exhausted itself on the first flight and was content to flash talons and lie on its back. We held onto it and moved on to the last member of the brood, but it was having none of it and, being more advanced than its siblings, surprised us by taking to the air, confidently securing a safe perch on the cliff opposite. There was nothing we could do so we took the second bird safely back to its natal cliff as the hen kestrel hung silently above us, taking it all in but keeping uncharacteristically quiet. We left her in charge.

The check on fledged young in the nesting territories brings to a close six months of fairly intense fieldwork, and although kestrels are an all-consuming passion, I have almost had enough by the end of July. Forty-five field days, between six and 12 visits to each territory, around 300 trees climbed and over 1,000 miles travelled will all have taken their toll. The cord is now cut and, apart from the inevitable writing-up, I revert to being an ordinary citizen who sees a kestrel hovering, notes it with pleasure and gets on with the rest of his life.

*Recently-fledged youngster in woodland setting, very unsure as to the next move*

By February, the batteries are fully recharged, raptor meetings and conferences have once more whetted the appetite and daylight hours are stretching nicely. The downside is that I have to start erecting nest boxes. I have around 60 boxes in nesting territories and each year some succumb to age or severe weather conditions and require repair or replacement. Normally two boxes are erected in each territory, partly to give the kestrels a choice but also to accommodate other avian predators, such as tawny owls and long-eared owls, which can compete for these luxury homes. The boxes are spaced well apart to minimize interaction between the species.

Kestrels readily take to this type of artificial nest and in Holland, much of the research work on the species is done using hundreds of nest boxes on poles to compensate for the lack of natural sites. In 2007, for example, the number of nest boxes occupied by kestrels was a staggering 604 out of 618 registered breeding sites, the others being in crows' nests and cavities

(Bijlsma 2007). In western Finland, Erkki Korpimaki (2008) and his team use similar large numbers of nest boxes to study kestrels and Tengmalm's owls (*Aegolius funereus*). Ronny Steen in Norway is currently studying over 100 pairs of kestrels using nest boxes and Bjorn Foyn's ringing group have 400 boxes in their study area.

Kestrels will take to most types of nest boxes, even using specially-designed chough nest boxes in Cornwall (*BTO News* 2008). One well-used A-frame barn owl box, erected by the Hawk and Owl Trust Worcestershire local group, had multiple use in 2007. First in were a pair of tawny owls which produced three young, to be followed two weeks after they had vacated the box by a pair of kestrels, which also fledged three young. Just to complete a very successful tenancy, a pair of barn owls which had previously nested 150 metres away, rearing four young, moved into the box and produced a second clutch of five eggs, two of which hatched. It was avian 'hot bedding' at its very best (*Peregrine* Spring 2008).

Over the years, kestrels have used open-fronted nest boxes on a regular basis but the design has one major shortcoming: they drain badly, even with drill holes in the base. In spells of heavy driving rain, the nest substrate becomes saturated and, unlike the crow's nest for which they are a substitute, they take a long time to dry out, which can delay laying. To overcome this defect I began to replace old boxes with a new oblong design which provided the requisite dry, sheltered nesting position well back in the box. One drawback of the new boxes is that they are particularly favoured by both tawny and barn owls, and while I have a soft spot for both species, I must admit to being a tad disappointed when the face peering out at me is owl-shaped. I've now reverted to the open-fronted design and the kestrels seem quite happy to use them. No matter what the design, the trees still have to be climbed and the boxes hauled up at a time of year when fieldwork fitness is not at its best and weather conditions are seldom conducive to long stays in the canopy.

*Early nest box design which was quickly modified*

*The new design of box attracted owls*

Discipline is vital, especially when it comes to carrying the correct equipment. For these early forays the tools of the trade are checked off before leaving the house – a folding garden pruning saw, a small hammer, nails, wire and staples, string, rope and gloves – and returned carefully to the shoulder bag after each climb. There is nothing worse than a long trek to a nesting territory with a nest box on the shoulder only to find that an essential piece of equipment is still in the car or, even worse, at home.

What I have found is that supporting the bottom of a box on a limb, as well as securing it to the trunk, can considerably prolong the box's life. The back support tends to rot first as dampness accelerates the decay. In some territories I am now on my third generation of boxes. One of my earliest boxes was still in use in 2009, at least a quarter of a century after it was installed, but the roof has finally caved in so a replacement will be necessary.

Renewing acquaintances with contacts, landowners, shepherds, foresters, farmers and householders is on the whole very enjoyable, but anxiety surfaces when changes take place, especially in ownership. The investment of time, effort and all important continuity can easily be in jeopardy if the new incumbents are not sympathetic. Thankfully with the kestrel this scenario is rare: almost all my contacts take great interest in the progress of the season and I make sure that they are kept well informed. Information on the recovery of a bird ringed on someone's land, an exceptional breeding year or details of other interesting sightings all help to cement relationships. Meticulous planning of access arrangements and exemplary behaviour, such as taking detours to avoid lambing sheep, are appreciated.

*Dovetailing with the farming cycle is essential*

The continuity of data, so critical in effective monitoring, was nearly thwarted in 2001 with the outbreak of foot and mouth and the consequent restrictions on access to the countryside. It severely tested the co-operation of even my most long-standing and keenest contacts but my perseverance was rewarded. Naturally, compliance with the precautions was absolute, and my boots were immersed in protective gunk so many times that rot had set in by the end of the season. Seventeen results were painstakingly teased from that season and the run of data remained unbroken.

The provision of information by shepherds and farmers on sightings of kestrels and interesting experiences always helps to build up a picture of what is happening. Pinpointing the activities of a pair at a wood or quarry can save valuable search time.

Early in the season there is little expectation of seeing kestrels in the upland study areas unless there is a spell of exceptionally mild weather. Indeed, on some visits it is a bonus to see a bird of any description. When the cone crop is substantial, welcome flocks of siskin and crossbill lighten the day and the early ravens are always liable to put in an appearance, checking me out from overhead. Sometimes, however, the signs are extremely positive. At one well-established upland territory, winter occupancy was always signaled by the scores of pellets and patches of droppings under favoured roosts in the roof supports of an open-sided corrugated iron barn.

*Signs of a well-used winter roost*

*Accumulation of pellets under a favoured sheltered perch*

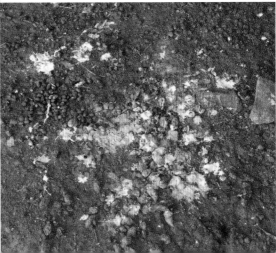

*Typical upland site with crow's nest in the shelter belt and roosts nearby*

Towards the middle of March, I start recording kestrels on territory as the birds begin to make serious attempts to establish themselves. On occasions, winter roosts do give good clues: signs such as droppings in an open barn or the distinctive whitewash under porches. This is the first of six pieces of information which are collected for each breeding attempt in the study areas, potentially involving around a dozen visits to each territory over a five month period. The other five statistics required are the date of the first egg being laid, the clutch size, hatching date, brood survival and fledging success. Getting in early is vital as pairs can fail at the pre-laying stage, leaving no visible signs, and data can easily be distorted if this is missed.

Establishing that birds are on territory and finding the nest site is by far the most challenging and enjoyable part of the season: it's the detective phase. You require nothing but your binoculars and your senses. A 'softly-softly' approach is most likely to be successful. The ideal situation is when you can view the territory from a distance and pick up the pair without even moving into the general nesting area. All you need to see initially are birds hunting, perched near or at a nest site, engaged in aerial battles with other raptors or crows or even displaying. Patience is everything, because hours of inactivity on the part of the birds are often followed by frenetic bursts of action when all can be revealed. It's the raptor way and to learn anything, you must conform.

*Early season check – female in residence*

*Unruffled, a female peers down at the intruder*

Kestrels select and compete for mates (they are mainly monogamous but polygamy has been recorded) and this is one of the few times in the season when the birds are very active and vocal as they display and strongly defend the core area round a nest site. They have an exclusive range at the beginning of the season, relaxing to larger overlapping ranges later in the cycle. Greater foraging is required at the beginning of the season when the field voles which make up their preferred diet are scarcer. The birds usually hunt within two kilometres of the nest site but will travel up to five kilometres.

High-pitched calling is often the first indication of a pair in residence and Tinbergen (1940) gives a comprehensive description of the range of calls at the pre-laying stage. Intruding kestrels are met with aggressive confrontation. If this posturing and bluff fails then actual fighting can occur, sometimes causing injury and even fatalities. Certainly in the south of Scotland there seems to be no lack of non-breeding birds available for recruitment into the population so early-season activity can be hectic.

The displays themselves are carried out to attract mates and to dissuade others. Activities include soaring above the nest site, soaring together, the cock diving at the stationary hen, chasing each other and even claw-grappling. There is a very diagnostic 'winnowing' flight, a sort of shivering motion of the wings as a bird approaches a potential nest site, and a 'V' flight, when the bird glides in with both wings upright above the head. Kestrels have even been recorded nibbling each other's claws in bouts of affection. There is definite fidelity at nest sites with some hens being recorded in the same territory for several years in succession. Similarly, the cock birds seem to have the same affinity with a territory and one bird nested for three seasons in the same area, pairing with a different hen each season and using a different nest site each time in my study area.

In the period preceding egg laying, copulation takes place at very regular intervals, on average at least once every 45 minutes for a number of days. The birds can begin copulation on a much more irregular basis a couple of months before eggs appear in the nest and, as Domenic Couzens (2007) so aptly put it, "If you've only got a life expectancy of four years or so, you might as well make the most of it". I have quite a few anecdotal records of kestrels copulating in autumn in fine weather at around the time when day length equates with Spring.

Once the initial burst of activity is over, the hen kestrel begins to hang around the nest site, relatively inactive, while her mate takes on the role of provider. This pre-laying lethargy helps to reduce her energy output and allows her to conserve her resources for the all-important egg-laying stage. She is quite visible at this time as she loafs around the nesting territory. This division of labour extends well into the breeding season, until the young are quite large and the hen feels able to hunt away from the site and contribute to the family food budget.

Even if you do not at first see any activity on one of these early visits, a cold search can yield clues as to the presence of a pair – the odd down feather on a branch or at the actual nest site, the remains of plucked prey, a build-up of fresh droppings or pellets. The pellets are very distinctive, measuring 20–40 mm in length and 10–25 mm in diameter. They are usually rounded at one end, tapering to a point at the other. When dry, the overall colour of the pellet is light grey, reflecting the fur of the main prey item, the short-tailed field vole. Freshly disgorged pellets are dark and have a wet appearance caused by mucus on the surface. When the wet pellets are ejected they often stick to branches and are obvious only when you get to the higher reaches of the canopy. If the canopy is particularly thick then you may not get any indication of pellets in the early part of the season. The kestrel pellet usually contains only small fragments of the prey items as the kestrel tears up its prey rather than swallowing it whole, as does its diurnal counterpart, the barn owl. Once your eye is in, it is amazing how you can pick up even tiny telltale signs. Kestrels also have a very distinct odour and on rare occasions, when hens have been in a nest box for some time, I have been able to confirm their presence simply by using my nose.

*Comparative sizes of raptor pellets – sea eagle, golden eagle, barn owl and kestrel*

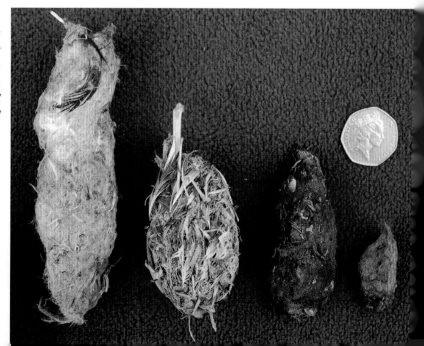

*Often nest debris like pellets and prey items stick to the upper branches*

It does pay to sneak around at this time and keep alert, as the hen can easily slip quietly away in front of you, especially if you are working the edge of a small plantation or shelter belt. A resting bird is also always liable to call out to a mate, often a soft intimate communication or, if she senses something happening near the nest, maybe in response to songbirds alarming, a subtle high-pitched worry call. It pays to tread warily. Your ears are a great asset at this time and windy days are a nightmare, robbing you of a valuable tool. It is a great bonus if your visit coincides with a food pass or even mating. Watching for the interaction of resident birds can also yield clues. Aerial tiffs between crows, buzzards or ravens going unchallenged by a resident kestrel in a core territory is often good circumstantial evidence of non-occupation. The combative kestrel punches well above its weight and does not hesitate to engage with larger birds.

It very often pays, when cold searching, to start checks at the corners of a wood or plantation as kestrels favour crow's nests in these locations, possibly because there is an advantage to be gained from a field of view in more than one direction. When leaving a wood after a fruitless search, remember too to stop regularly and give a backward scan. If the birds have slipped off without your noticing, you can sometimes spot them sneaking back.

One thing in the fieldworker's favour is that good-quality territories are likely to be occupied year after year by kestrels, allowing you to build up a useful information base of potential nest sites, roosts and loafing areas. The best example I have is on the Dam site for which I have unbroken data since 1973. It was no great surprise when reading through the late Donald Watson's meticulous notes that there was a reference to kestrels breeding there in 1960. Sadly, it was robbed in that year. In 1964, he recorded a brood of four on 1 July, the pair having a penchant for birds if the list of prey remains is anything to go by – lapwing, partridge, blackbird, greenfinch, chaffinch and starling.

Once it is established that a pair is on territory, you might assume that it is a mere formality to pin down the actual nest site. That is by no means the case. Despite some misinformation in books stating that kestrels build their own nests, this small falcon is in reality dependent upon having a soft substrate which can be excavated using its feet to form a shallow nest cup or scrape into which the hen lays its clutch. This can be the base of an old crow's nest, a soft ledge on a cliff or building, a hole in a tree or a luxury custom-built nest box.

Nest site in building

Extensive use is made of previous year's crow's stick platform

*Traditional cliff ledge site*

*Kestrels readily take to nest boxes*

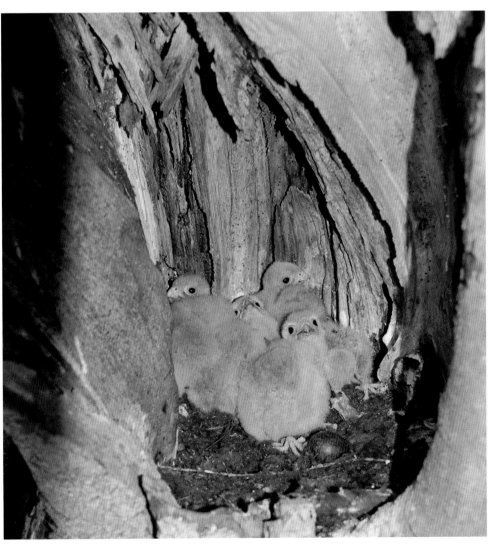

*Holes in trees are often used*

*Classic nest scrape on a crag ledge*

*As incubation proceeds there is a build-up of debris giving the illusion of a built nest*

As the season progresses, the accumulation of pellets, nibbled vegetation, prey items, feathers and other debris do give the impression of a constructed nest but at the onset of the cycle, the base is bare substrate. I therefore put a layer of well-decomposed woodland litter, scraped from below conifer trees, in the bottom of the nest box to simulate a natural surface.

There is no distinct pattern of usage of sites within a territory. A site may be used for years, as with one of the Dam sites mentioned above, so it is just a matter of walking in and recording. At the other end of the spectrum are those pairs which carry out nest inspections in a territory, scrape out several sites, and hang around for three to four weeks, or even two months in one instance, before deciding that the conditions are right for the first egg to be laid. This can involve a lot of repetitive climbing.

Crows' nests can be very difficult to find even in small shelter belt woodlands and it pays to take careful note of active nests in the previous season. In 2000, it was not until the end of July and after six fruitless visits to the Magpie Wood that I located the crow platform and three well-grown chicks. The stick nest, fully 50 feet above the ground, was wedged between two trunks of a double-headed conifer, and all telltale debris had fallen into the crook of the tree. Only dogged patience and a long vigil waiting for a feeding visit by an adult eventually allowed me to track it down.

Once an occupied nesting territory has been identified, it becomes a matter of pride to find the nest. Even if nest boxes have been erected in the territory, there is no guarantee that the kestrels will choose them. It is, though, well worth checking them all out every year as one box remained empty for seven years before finally tempting a pair to use it.

Other species, notably the heron and the raven, are well into their breeding cycle by March or early April, and both birds are key members of the supporting cast which adds immensely to the pleasure of fieldwork. When I find them nesting close to kestrels, I make a note of their progress too, and pass the information on to the appropriate people. Their impact on the kestrels rarely goes beyond some aerial bantering but there is competition from other species for nest sites. Barn owls, long-eared owls and tawny owls all covet the nest boxes and the long-eared owl will also readily make use of crow platforms. Friction between kestrels and long-eared owls is minimal as the latter's numbers are very low and nesting is sporadic in the study areas. The other two owls, though, are quite able to displace kestrels, which is why I always put up at least two boxes in a territory. Squatters like these just have to be accepted as part of the game, and at least I don't get pine martens using the boxes as Mike Canham, a member of the Highland Raptor Study Group, does in the Highlands. Grey and red squirrels, too, have a liking for boxes and pack them with sticks and a lined core.

*Occasionally barn owls and kestrels compete for nest sites but usually they tolerate close neighbours*

*The tawny owl usually comes out on top in competition for nest sites*

The period before and during laying is one of the most demanding stages in the breeding cycle, as both the cock and hen kestrel have high energy expenditure. While the male provisions the female, she builds up large quantities of fat while forming eggs. It's not hard to see why she needs to: a full clutch of eggs will weigh 130–140 grams, almost half the weight of the female herself.

The eggs are laid in the mornings at two-day intervals and incubation usually starts with the third egg. This is also a critical time for me, as once the first egg is laid and the date recorded, a result of some kind is guaranteed and I can work out the timescale for the remainder of the visits. As an amateur with a full time job, this time management has been critical to making the most effective use of valuable field time. My records show the two earliest eggs as having been laid on 17 March 2000 and 27 March 1997, both in very open springs with minimal adverse weather conditions and good vole numbers.

One intriguing fact linked to the timing of the cycle is that the first egg each season was often laid in one particular territory in my study area, a small shelter belt in the middle of sheep pasture, which supported a heronry. Although not holding the record for the earliest laying, it was amazing that despite the changeover of hens and the similarity of adjacent territories, it was invariably the first. In 2010, the hen laid the first egg in the last week of March during a spell of very bad weather and was more than two weeks earlier than any other pair.

Another visit is needed shortly after the first laying to verify the full clutch size, which is usually four to six eggs, although I have had a couple of sevens and one eight over the past four decades. For several years, in selected territories, the adults were caught in order to try to estimate the turnover of the population. This was done under license from Scottish Natural Heritage and was a very exciting part of the season. Results were immediate, and I would catch either a new bird, a previous year's adult bird which I or someone else had ringed, or one that I or someone else had ringed as a nestling. To ring and measure a bird gives the rare privilege of seeing an adult bird at close quarters.

*Cock bird trapped as part of the adult turnover project*

The ethics of catching a bird at the nesting stage or of checking for the first egg did worry me at first. Now, though, I feel very confident that the fieldwork has not affected the end result for the highly resilient kestrel: the first adult caught was retrapped for five years, failing to produce young only once when the nest site was flooded, and I have not seen any negative results from checking clutches early. On my visits to the nest site at the beginning of the season, time is of the essence: I need to get in quickly, do what is necessary and get out again as fast as possible. There was never enough time to get a large enough sample size of hens so the work was discontinued.

Even from a small sample, though, it was clear that there was a quick turnover of females, although one or two of the birds did return for several years. Six females bred in the Dam between 1980 and 1992 while in the Gable End in a ten-year period, a staggering eight females bred. This quick turnover of adults is not unexpected in a small falcon species such the kestrel, in which an adult reaching four years has done extremely well.

*Turnover of breeding females 1980–1992*

| | 80 | 81 | 82 | 83 | 84 | 85 | 86 | 87 | 88 | 89 | 90 | 91 | 92 |
|---|---|---|---|---|---|---|---|---|---|---|---|---|---|
| 6 Dam | A | A | A | B | nb | C | D | C | C | D | E | E | F |
| 6 Limekilns | | | | | A | B | A | C | D | E | F | nb | nb |
| 6 Quarry | | | A | B | nb | nb | C | D | E | D | F | nb | nb |
| 8 Gable end | | | A | B | nb | C | nc | C | D | E | F | G | H |
| 5 Meadowhead | | | | | | A | nb | B | B | C | nb | D | E |

nb = no birds read; nc = no birds caught

If close-up work is planned for the season, then this is the time to set up the hides. In the early days I found that hide work was critical in getting to know the kestrel. Being so close to the birds for long periods of time helped me to build up my knowledge of patterns of behaviour and the meaning of different calls, all of which helped interpretation during fieldwork. Knowing the signals can help shorten the process of nest site location. I tune in to food passes which are normally quite vocal, and hear the female making contact calls to the male from the nest, which often happens if she knows he is around and not out hunting. The reaction of other species to the presence of kestrels can also be extremely useful.

I clearly remember one particular incident while working in a hide:

*A Reptile Moment*
*7 June 1991*

The day had begun without great promise and a late start dictated a conservative target of five territories in the afternoon and early evening. By this time the work tends to be very straightforward, the searching and pinpointing of breeding sites now behind me. By the time I reached the Quarry I was on a roll, four pairs progressing well and full data collected. A hide had been set up a few weeks previously on a rather precarious cliff face near a ledge site which had housed five newly-hatched chicks on the last visit. Unfortunately the hide was on a downward sloping bank, bare of soil, and it had to be anchored using the largest stones I could hoist up the slope. Still, it had survived so far and the fact that

*Kestrels for Company*

*Close encounter of the reptile kind*

the hen kestrel left the nest at my approach confirmed acceptance. All five chicks were well and while she objected vocally at a safe distance I set up the camera and slipped in while she was distracted by a passing crow. The next hour and a half was a cocktail of discomfort and frustration as the hen settled down to preen and bask in the early evening sunlight just out of lens range, occasionally taking off to deter a persistent cuckoo which was working the quarry edge.

I suddenly became aware of a trickle of small stones and dust coming into the side of the hide. Concentration levels in such a confined space are heightened and any variation or change in status is instantly detected. I was not prepared for the next few seconds as the last of the mini avalanche was followed by a 12-inch reptile which slithered down the side of my left leg. I could feel the sweat running down my back and it certainly wasn't from the heat. It was impossible to flee the hide as I'd probably break my neck so I stayed motionless as the male adder made its way leisurely round the front base of the hide. As it touched my boot I gave an almighty kick which propelled the unfortunate animal out through the thin fern cover at the front of the hide which thankfully had not fitted tight to the ground. It landed six feet below, righted itself and went on its way in much better shape than the rather moist human it had encountered.

Oblivious to the mini drama, the hen kestrel was still bickering at the cuckoo so I waited till the first opportune moment, a food pass round the corner, and left. It had happened so quickly, yet it seemed in slow motion. I shudder to think what would have happened if the adder had come in the other side and crossed my hand which rested on the ground for extra support.

This was not my only close encounter with an adder. Early one morning I was sitting watching a wood as a distant pair of kestrels displayed, moving in and out of their selected tree. So intent was I on the kestrels that I had failed to notice the adder coiled on an adjacent tussock of grass as it absorbed the heat from the emerging sun's rays. Luckily for me it was very lethargic and hadn't moved at all when I settled down – nor when I hastily moved position.

Incubation usually begins after the third egg and takes between 28 and 30 days. Surprisingly, it is almost a lull in the proceedings, an easy time for cock, hen and fieldworker alike. I use the opportunity to take stock of the season to date, make a repeat search of those territories which have produced a blank early on and also to monitor failed pairs just in case of a repeat clutch. Although the kestrel is single-brooded, a repeat clutch will occasionally be laid if the first breeding attempt fails and the first clutch is lost at an early stage in the cycle. Failure to re-check could distort the true outcome of the season. Most of the time it is just going through the motions and I instinctively know I'm at a dead end when a buzzard is soaring and calling above a wood, crows swing up to mob it and no little warrior puts in an appearance.

Perseverance occasionally pays off. One wood had been checked on five visits with not so much as a glimpse of a kestrel, let alone a breeding attempt, yet the territory rarely went unused. One last climb on a late round of visits again proved fruitless but as I stood catching my breath at the bottom of the tree, a female kestrel flew, calling, into the very next tree. The burst of calls indicated a brood present. The tree was a huge grizzly sitka and, although there was no sign at the base, the usual nest debris became more noticeable as I climbed higher. So thick were the branches that nothing had filtered to ground level. Near the top, five very mature nestlings stared at me over the lip of the crow's nest. Catching them for ringing would have spelled disaster as they would certainly have exploded from the nest with little chance of my getting them back, so I had to be satisfied with recording the brood size.

The hen does most of the domestic work: the cock bird will come in and cover the clutch after an off-site prey exchange but he does not generally like to stay on the eggs too long. It must be a very long day for the hen and she constantly moves round, turning the eggs, dozing but perking up at the least noise. A soft calling is occasionally to be heard, possibly an attempt to check if the mate is nearby. Visits from the male can be well spaced and I can still remember the discomfort of a six-hour wait for one food pass and one photograph. I have on five occasions actually climbed to a box and had the hen stay put.

On one occasion in Culzean Country Park on the South Ayrshire coast where I worked, I was lucky enough to have my camera to hand. Making the most of this precious moment, I extended myself to the last rung of the ladder and, with excruciatingly slow movements, positioned myself with one hand on the camera and one on the ivy next to the box. I fired off a few shots, retreated gingerly and left her still in charge of the clutch. It was a very special moment. I actually caught one female asleep on a clutch on an exceptionally hot day, while two others were successfully surprised due to windy conditions masking my climb. All these situations were in hole-type locations: three in nest boxes, one in a tree and another in a limekiln.

*Cock birds only take over incubation duties for short periods to relieve the hen*

*Caught napping*

Hatching is the second real pressure point for the breeding pair and early warning comes from the cheeping of the young inside the egg. The egg tooth is critical and it's quite amazing how precise a cut the emerging chick executes to remove the top of the egg. It is an exhausting task and, still damp, the chick often collapses from the effort, lying in the bottom of the nest until its white down dries out. It is hard to equate this tiny bundle, weighing only 14–16 grams, with the pocket battleship which will, in just a month's time, be able to defend itself with vigour.

*Hen kestrel which decided to stay put while the clutch was checked*

*Egg tooth – essential tool for hatching*

*First sign of the struggle to hatch*

*Interlocked egg shells can prevent a safe hatch*

Accidents can happen at this time and one of the most unfortunate is when the shell, still moist from a recently hatched sibling, accidentally bonds onto the top of another egg. The double shell is just too thick for the chick to penetrate and it will invariably perish. My objectivity is always compromised on the rare occasion when I witness this: should I intervene or not?

On another occasion I had an even more difficult decision to make. While watching a kestrel pair which had nested in an old raven's nest in a quarry, the hen came off the nest to collect food from the cock bird and inadvertently pulled off a newly-hatched chick. The white bundle fell down the rock face and into the long grass below. I shot over and after a few minutes found the resilient chick, still alive and apparently unhurt. The dilemma was that I had no climbing gear with me and the nest was on a fairly inaccessible ledge. Kestrel safely tucked in my pocket, I climbed the face and managed to get opposite the ledge but the gap

*Three recently-hatched young and two chipping eggs*

between the two ledges was about five feet. Decision made, I lobbed the young over the gap for its second flight and a safe landing among its siblings. The target, to be fair, was quite large, as ravens' nests are, and the soft wool lining made the risk acceptable. Nonetheless I climbed down with a mixture of satisfaction and relief. Two and a half weeks later, the adventurer was ringed with the rest of the brood and fledged successfully.

The brood usually hatches over a 4–5 day period but synchronous hatches have been recorded. Inclement weather at this time can be fatal, especially if food is difficult to obtain. Caching of food, either nearby in a banking, round the nest rim or at the back of a nest box has been recorded and this helps enhances the survival chances in the key first few days. This practice has also been recorded outside the breeding season and on one occasion on the Mull of Galloway, a female kestrel repeatedly caught and stuffed prey into a hole in a cliff (Paul Tarling, pers comm). Non-hatched eggs do remain in the nest and are often still present at the end of the season.

During the first couple of weeks the hen broods, feeds and protects the chicks and it is rare for the cock bird to spend much time at the nest site. He accelerates his hunting and his skill, especially during inclement weather, will go a very long way in determining the success or failure of the breeding attempt.

*Cock bird startled to find the hen off the nest*

There is always an exception to the rule, exemplified by one remarkable male in 2008. A routine breeding attempt in a nest box in the garden of Douglas and Vivien Bremner, who live near Castle Douglas, was progressing well until, on 22 May, the female was found badly injured, its head bloodied and one eye missing. Sadly her injuries, probably inflicted by a tawny owl, were so bad that she was put down by the local SSPCA inspector.

And so it was decision time. Should the ten-day old young be removed and hand reared, or should nature take its course, at least initially, with supporting feeding? The latter strategy was adopted after telephone calls from Canna where I was on holiday. Vivien religiously placed small pieces of steak just inside the box which contained five young and an addled egg.

*The best of steak for this brood*

Incredibly, the male used the Bremners' generosity to great effect. The young developed, were duly ringed and successfully fledged, but not before appearing on the BBC Scotland evening news programme. For the male to have taken on the burden of both hunting and looking after the brood was quite exceptional and on 25 June, Douglas and Vivien had the satisfaction of seeing all five dust bathing on the road up to their house.

Tinbergen, in his study of breeding kestrels (1940), recorded one similar occasion when a male kestrel tore up food for the young after the hen had been killed. The young were at 13 days and still could not feed unaided.

The food requirement for an adult is around 40 grams per day, equivalent to, say, two average-sized voles or a juvenile starling, but when you have four to six voracious chicks then the pressure is on. The initial control at feeding times is very apparent with the hen delicately tearing off small pieces of the prey and gently proffering them to the young in turn. This deteriorates into a scrum towards the end of the brood period with food deposited by both adults and the young left to sort it out for themselves. I've seen a 14 day old chick grab a small vole from the hen as she alighted on the nest rim and swallow it whole, just like an owl. The chick struggled for at least five minutes before eventually swallowing the rodent and on several occasions it looked to be close to choking.

*When the young are small, feeding is very controlled*

Voles are definitely the preferred prey item and provide the bulk of the diet where they occur. Other items are taken according to their abundance in relation to voles but the catholic kestrel does have a very extensive prey range including insects and other invertebrates and other small mammals and birds up to the size of a lapwing. Birds are a summer bulk item, especially in June and July when there is a flush of inexperienced pipits, skylarks and starlings available. One of the most unusual prey items I've recorded was in a nest at fairly high altitude in an upland study area – the collection of feathers scattered round the nest could only have come from an escaped budgerigar. To preserve local public relations I kept this information strictly between the kestrel and myself.

*Telltale budgie feathers betray an opportunist hunter*

The ideal time to ring the young kestrels is at about two and a half weeks old when the legs and feet have developed sufficiently to ensure that the metal split ring will stay on and not work its way over the claws and cause unacceptable distress and damage. Tackling a brood later when they are feathered, fearless and ferocious is not recommended, especially when they are 50 feet up a tree or on a difficult cliff face. A brood of six kestrels flicking onto their backs and presenting an array of talons must be quite intimidating to some predators. It is a very dynamic and enjoyable phase as you are now tree fit, know where to go, get a chance to examine the birds at close quarters and are beginning to get a very good idea of how the season is panning out.

The reaction of the adults to the presence of someone at the nest varies, especially during ringing when the young can make a terrible racket. Usually the birds fly around calling at a respectable distance, the male often disappearing. It is rare for them to come in close but it does happen. At one quarry site, I was ringing the young *in situ* on a ledge when a whoosh of wings was the only warning before I was clipped by an adult. At another site, a nest box on a BT Cellnet tower, the female landed on the structure only 15 feet above and berated me continuously as the young were ringed. The nest box had been erected by BT who also put up a tit box below, presumably to provide a food source!

Ringing always throws up incidents. Imagine the predicament when, balanced on a narrow ledge in a quarry, ringing a brood of four quite lively young, one rebel scoots past me and perches on my extended leg. Not as flexible as I used to be, it took fully ten minutes of delicate manoeuvring to recapture it.

One of the most bizarre incidents was at a nest box site about 25 feet up a spruce tree. I was positioned ready to ring the five birds in the box when a lizard suddenly scuttled from among

*The ideal size for ringing – the leg takes a ring
and the bird does not fight back*

*Gael with two sprightly young ready for ringing*

*At the later brood stage the young are perfectly capable of defending themselves*

[Left] BT Cellnet kestrel nest box with prey items housed below!

[Bottom left] Unusually the hen kestrel came in close and watched proceedings

[Bottom right] The hen kestrel perched on top of the nest box was reluctant to move

*Does a lizard have nine lives too?*

the brood and began to try and climb up the wall of the box. I caught it and, on examination, found that it had half its tail eaten and a puncture mark, presumably from a talon, in its belly. Its zest for survival was impressive so I popped it in my pocket and released it below the tree once I had completed the ringing, watching it immediately race for cover in the nearby stone dyke. It was not the first lizard I had found as a prey item, although in two cases they had been discarded and were lying dead below the nest site.

At one of the long-base style boxes at Culzean the ladder didn't quite reach the side door so I had to stretch my arm in from below and feel for the chicks. All four birds were safely caught and brought down to be processed. It was Rosie, my wife, who suddenly pointed up to the box where a fifth youngster had appeared at the entrance, peering down at us, wondering where its siblings had gone. Much banter ensued as the clutch size had been reported at four so when I'd caught the requisite number I naturally assumed that was that. Presumably when the nest was checked at mid-incubation the female had dislodged one egg when she departed and pulled it back into the fold when she returned.

Ageing and sexing young kestrels in the nest is not an exact science as although they can be aged approximately by using wing length, this parameter cannot be used to sex them. The measurements of males and females overlap considerably. However, the colour and pattern of the upper tail coverts can be used to sex individuals if the chicks are three weeks or older and have wing lengths greater than 138 mm. Females have brown upper tail coverts with broad dark brown bands while males have grayish tail coverts with smaller bands. This is, however, by no means totally foolproof. For more details check *Raptors: a Field Guide to Survey and Monitoring* (Hardey *et al.* 2006).

*Two nearly-fledged young showing definite male and female plumage on the upper tail coverts*

The aim of the ringing programme is to find out what happens to the young after they leave the nest and disperse. How far do they travel, what is the survival rate and do they return to their natal sites? The recovery rate is extremely low and I'm very lucky to receive two or three outcomes annually from the British Trust for Ornithology after ringing 50–80 nestlings each season. Every effort has been made to ring broods in the same territories each year rather than to take a scattergun approach by ringing broods outside the study area. The results have been quite illuminating.

*Happy feet! But not if you are handling them*

There is a random dispersal of young in late July and early August with birds going in all directions. Up until late autumn, recoveries included birds found at Aberdeen, Newtonmore, Isle of May, Ireland, Sussex, Devon and a patriotic bird which died at Bannockburn. Some birds moved very quickly, one reaching South Humberside by 1 August, a distance of 317 kilometres.

The initial dispersal is followed by a predominantly southwards movement, birds reaching the south of England by October and northern Europe by November. Of the 37 recoveries in the first winter, all but one had moved south. The furthest-travelled bird was ringed at Culzean on the South Ayrshire coast on 19 June and had reached Tenerife by 11 October, killing itself by flying into a pylon – a very creditable 3,076 kilometres in quick time and to date the longest distance recorded for a Scottish kestrel on migration. The only recorded bird to reach the African continent from Scotland was ringed in the Grampian region and was found in Morocco, a journey of 2,439 kilometers. Movements like this and the Culzean bird are exceptional.

*Kestrels regularly use the platforms as stepping stones on migration*

Other birds were recovered in northern France, Spain, the Netherlands and several in Ireland. This movement towards the Continent was not confined to birds in their first winter: one in France was in its fourth winter and the longest surviving bird, found dead in Suffolk, was in its eleventh winter. Small samples, of course, but pointers nonetheless.

From BTO figures, sixteen records exist of birds recovered in Scotland from abroad and, not surprisingly, the majority are from Scandinavia, fitting well with the data collected from the North Sea Bird Club (Riddle 1985). Kestrels regularly use the oil installations as stopovers on migration in spring and autumn. One of the Ayrshire-ringed birds was recovered as a breeding bird in Norway the following season. It was possibly caught up in the company of birds returning to Norway from western Europe in the spring.

By the end of the third week the pattern at the nest has changed. The hen still keeps a close watch on proceedings but from a distance, as she is constantly pestered for food when she lands on the nest. Food is dropped in by both adults and I have seen ten voles deposited in a six-hour spell. Another fieldworker has recorded 28 voles in one day. In times of plenty the voles can certainly accumulate at the nest and I have recorded 33 voles and a couple of woodmice piled up around five very cramped young with bulging crops. I could smell the pile of bodies well before reaching the nest ledge. The adults must have struck a very rich vein.

*Thirty three small mammals were piled up in the nest – the aroma was pungent*

A melee normally accompanies the dropping-off of prey at the nest, followed by one nestling successfully acquiring the food and keeping the others at bay by turning its back on them and mantling the prize, hunching over the prey and using its outstretched wings to block any side attacks. Unless they are extremely hungry the others settle down quite quickly and, of course, when the next delivery occurs, the most determined effort is made by those which have been without food the longest. Purely from a survival standpoint it is simply not in their interest to tussle and struggle too much when there are up to six birds on a narrow ledge or on a crow platform which is getting flatter by the day.

As the season progresses the nest site changes dramatically in character. In the early clutch and post- hatching phases there is little sign of droppings in the immediate vicinity, although pellets do filter down to the ground below and the odd moulted feather can be a giveaway. The hen begins to moult during incubation and feathers are often present in the nest debris. Nest site security is paramount at the clutch and early brood period, but as the young begin to lose their down and become hard-feathered, they can put up a spirited defence against predators.

Squalid is not too strong a word for the site towards the end of the brood period as pellets, droppings and an assortment of inedible prey parts attract hosts of flies. The aroma is very distinctive. Climbing trees to access nest sites can be messy. Droppings are deposited over the nest rim and when checking nests at this time, the higher you climb, the messier it gets. There can also be deterioration of the actual nest site itself, especially if it's an old crow's nest, and collapses have happened with fatal consequences. On several occasions the young have been literally hanging on just prior to leaving the nest.

Between feeding visits, the level of activity in the nest ranges from the young dozing peacefully to bouts of frenetic exercise as individuals hone basic skills. Stabbing strikes at bones or wing remains imitate the killing action, while wing stretching or flapping exercises become more frequent as the end of the brood time comes around. A lot of time is spent staring out at the surrounding vista, presumably building up a local map which will be vital when they finally fledge. If something interests them or comes into their line of vision, their heads bob up and down and all attention is focused on the object.

The third and final pressure point in the cycle comes with fledging. As the young become more confident they begin to explore their environs, moving onto adjacent branches if it's a tree nest or around a cliff face or building. Their inexperience can often be their downfall as a slip at this time can result in a fall which may not hurt but which makes them easy prey for ground predators such as foxes. I watched one brancher exploring an ivy-covered cliff and taking three quarters of an hour to scrabble in panic back up to the safety of the nest cavity after it had been too ambitious in its wanderings.

*Branchers move about the immediate vicinity of the nest*

*The young quickly become habituated to my presence*

To get the chance to watch a brood at this stage can be very rewarding. At the end of June 2004, I visited a ruined tower house which had a kestrel pair in residence using an inaccessible hole high in the masonry. Keen to get fledgling data, I slipped into the main area and just stood with my back to the wall among the chest-high nettles and elder scrub which had long since replaced the people. The young kestrels were out of the nest and scattered round the upper walls. In the next three hours I did nothing but observe as they gradually accepted my presence and got on with life.

Activity came in sudden energetic bursts, two or even three birds coming together, sometimes running over the stonework, at other times making short tentative flights. Adventurous journeys onto the top of the wall would invariably provoke bombing attacks from the local swallows which sent them ducking and weaving down to lower levels again. They seemed keen to seek out vantage points and sat staring out into the surrounding fields, heads bobbing as other birds flew by.

The youngest bird never ventured to the top but stayed quite low, lacking the confidence of its siblings. The nesting territory could have been purpose-built for these birds: with routes easily accessible across the walls, perches all over the place, shelter and vantage points, it made for an ideal safe training area. They were very relaxed, spent a lot of time preening and were not averse to dozing off. One bird even approached close and gave me a thorough looking over.

All this changed when the adults came in, only twice in the three hours. The male, businesslike as usual, didn't even notice me. He just called, presented a vole to the youngster which got to his position first, and then was off. The chosen one immediately scuttled into a recess, mantled the prey item and gave the cold shoulder to another bird which, to be honest, did not try to press home its attentions. They all seemed well fed and in excellent feather condition.

The hen was quite different. In she came with a vole, landed on a ledge, delivered the prey, picked up my presence immediately and left at pace calling loudly. The young hardly reacted and once the half-hearted squabble for the vole had subsided, they retreated to their favourite perches.

Such was their confidence that I was able to use the camera without disturbing them in the least, which came as quite a bonus. When I slipped away they did not even react. I had become part of the scenery.

It is a vulnerable time which can be exploited by avian predators. Chris Rollie, the Chairman of the Dumfries & Galloway raptor study group and a close friend, had pinpointed a pair of kestrels nesting in a quarry which I had not previously visited. No sooner had I parked the car at the entrance when there was a terrific commotion. Out flew a female peregrine clutching a struggling young kestrel in its talons. The kestrel was screaming as were both adult birds as they pursued the departing peregrine. The kestrels doggedly hung in on the larger raptor's tail, eventually forcing it to drop the unfortunate youngster in a huge area of hillside bracken. A search of the area proved fruitless but it was unlikely that the bird had survived its ordeal. Back at the quarry the other three young were cowering near the lip of the rock face. Caught unawares due to their inexperience, one of the brood had paid the ultimate penalty.

Gradually the young become more adventurous and spread out. The adults begin to feed them away from the nest and this is a very vocal time. The nest is still, though, the focus of attention and they return to it regularly to roost, doze, or in response to adult alarm calls. For the fieldworker this is a vital but difficult time as trying to complete the jigsaw by recording the number of fledged young can be frustrating. Broods around buildings, cliffs and quarries are difficult enough but woodland families are a nightmare, as the birds constantly change positions round the woodland edge and never come into sight at one time. One of the great pleasures at the end of the season is watching newly-fledged young, short-tailed and unsteady on their pins, as they take their first steps into the big wide world.

*A screamer attracts the attention of an incoming adult*

It's also the time when the close relationship between kestrel and fieldworker is severed for another year. Back to viewing at a distance, writing up notes, filling in forms and waiting for ringing recoveries: the silence of the post-season.

*The final check*

The kestrels remain in family groups for some time, the adults provisioning the brood initially, gradually teaching them to hunt by dropping food and by hunting in their company. Chris Rollie had the great pleasure one day of watching a pair continually dropping voles or throwing them up in the air for the young to catch. The juveniles can also be seen on the ground, moving about with their ungainly gait, pecking at the ground, presumably looking for insects.

One phenomenon which can be spectacular is when family parties merge into loose amalgamations in habitats where food is abundant. A line of 15–25 birds hanging in the air above a ridge in late summer and early autumn is not uncommon. On 7 August 1981, the late Dick Roxburgh saw 15 kestrels in the air in one area and 30 in another, while in 1987 Donald Watson recorded 40 birds visible at once over an extensive area of newly-planted conifers. That must have been a wonderful sight. It was the golden age for both kestrel and short-eared owl in southwest Scotland: a kestrelfest.

# 2

## *Villains and Ploys*

Enjoyable though annual monitoring is, the injection of a fresh project can add spice to a new season. The Forestry Commission provided the stimulus for the 1992 season when, in early December 1991, the South Scotland Conservancy Council called together all current fieldworkers in an attempt to co-ordinate the ornithological research taking place on their ground. This initiative in itself was to be applauded, but they had taken an even more positive step by appointing one of their Forest Rangers, Geoff Shaw, to the post of Leading Ranger for Bird Conservation in Galloway. Quite a mouthful of a title but Geoff, a member of our Raptor Study Group with a special interest in the barn owl, was well equipped to co-ordinate and carry out work on a range of key forest bird species.

One of the questions which had been intriguing me was how kestrels would respond to the vast open areas which were being created as the first crops of sitka spruce were being harvested. I submitted a project to set up a nest box scheme on the fringes of a newly-felled sector of the Carrick forest to assess the kestrels' reaction to this second-phase development of the forest.

These restocked areas, to use the correct terminology, were quite different in character from the initial planting on ploughed hill pasture. The debris from the felling operations had not been burned. Instead, the tangle of cut branches had been pushed into huge mounds running down the hillside, leaving broad bands of clear ground in which the sitka had been planted.

One very important factor in choosing this area was that the previous history of colonisation by kestrels had been well documented. Robin Heaney, the Senior Ranger, and I had carried out surveys in the 1960s and early 1970s. It had followed the classic pattern of a dramatic increase in the number of kestrel breeding territories from five to 15 at the early planting stages, followed by a decline to several pairs on the forest perimeter as the canopy closed and hunting areas diminished and then disappeared.

A meeting was set up on site with Commission staff and, after close scrutiny of the felling programme, the general areas were chosen and the project was given the green light. Close liaison was set up with Robin and Geoff and, during February, ten boxes were positioned along the line of well-established sitka on the edge of newly-planted ground. There was the potential for four new nesting territories with the option of more boxes the following year. A great bonus

*Robin Heaney erecting one of the Carrick Forest nest boxes*

*Michael Callan with a nest box on the edge of the newly-planted ground*

was that this new area bordered the Rock study plot, so the economies of time management were very favourable.

Raptors were sighted regularly on forest visits, although buzzards were more in evidence than kestrels. Several kestrels were seen hunting within the forest but I was willing to accept that the first year could be barren as the grass was still threadbare and lacking in voles. By the end of April, the boxes were in position and it turned out to be a successful start, with one box occupied by a pair of kestrels rearing five young. The following year was equally encouraging, with two pairs of kestrels breeding and a couple of the boxes occupied by tawny owls.

The highlight, though, was a pair of long-eared owls which used a box on the very edge of the forest. That was a bonus in itself, but when a hide was erected and a camera trained on the box, I was treated to the bird's impressive aggressive display. Reacting to its own image in the lens it puffed itself up, spread its wings and attempted to displace the ghost intruder.

Everything was going nicely to plan and in 1994 a third pair of kestrels settled into a territory next to good feeding in a restock plot and again took advantage of a nest box. The first indication of something untoward came on 3 May when a hen kestrel was found, freshly plucked, below the nest box she had been using in the Wader Wood. Only the feathers remained: no carcass, no head, no legs, no chewed ends of feathers, no mammal or raptor droppings and no disturbed ground to give a clue to the predator. What was intriguing was that all the primary feathers, notoriously difficult to remove, had been plucked from the body. The incident was duly photographed and logged.

In the next two weeks five more plucked kestrel remains, including the three Carrick Forest birds, were discovered under nest boxes. The possibility of a goshawk was beginning to loom: a hen had been recorded in the area the previous year. It is well documented in ornithological literature that goshawks will prey on other raptors and they certainly have the strength to

*A pair of long-eared owls were early residents*

*The plucked remains of a hen kestrel at the front of the nest box tree*

*Another plucked hen and one of the young kestrels which had starved*

pluck large prey clean, are secretive by nature and even to the experienced eye can easily go undetected.

Incredibly, a second kestrel hen which had moved into the vacant Wader Wood territory and laid a clutch of five also fell victim to the predator. Confirmation came on 17 June when, on a final check of the forest territories, a male goshawk flew out of a ride and along the road in front of the car before veering off into the anonymity of the sitka.

This villain puts the peregrine to shame when it comes to annihilating the kestrel. Its impact was enormous. As it turned out, the kestrel wasn't the only raptor to suffer. Two of Geoff Shaw's merlin pairs failed as one of the adults in each pair was killed by 'a bigger raptor'. The signs were very similar to those found at the kestrel sites. Sadly, the kestrel has not been very successful in the Carrick Forest since 1994 and only a couple of successful breeding attempts have been recorded.

A couple of years later I visited a goshawk nest site with Geoff Shaw. It was quite an eye opener. As we approached the nest site, the hen was calling outrageously loudly and the signs of occupation were everywhere. The nest itself, positioned on the side of a larch tree, was huge and to my eye almost as big a stick platform as an eagle's, although not nearly as deep. Droppings were splashed all around the vicinity and the remains of prey items – red squirrel, pigeon and possibly a jay – were scattered on the tops of the uprooted base plates of surrounding trees. Not a plucked kestrel in sight but, no show without punch, the hen goshawk was suddenly assailed by a pair of suicidal kestrels which kept nipping at the larger bird's tail as she sailed over the canopy. The goshawk was largely indifferent to the agitated kestrels which gave up after five minutes. The size and sheer power of the bird was breathtaking and I suspected that the two kestrels would pay a heavy price if they persisted in ruffling those feathers. Geoff later confirmed that a pile of kestrel feathers had appeared on one of the root plates. The goshawk has been described as a sparrowhawk on steroids with attitude, and I wouldn't argue with that.

A very enlightening paper by Steve Petty *et al.* (2003) documents the decline of kestrels in the large coniferous Keilder Forest in northern England, giving a graphic picture of the scale of the impact of a so-called super predator. The numbers of kestrels and short-eared owls which hunt voles by day fell as a number of goshawks, probably originated from stock released by hawk keepers, first colonized the area and then became a breeding population. The mainly nocturnal tawny and long-eared owls did not suffer as badly.

The most significant statistic was that 4% of 5,511 goshawk prey items was made up of six raptor species but that more kestrels were killed than the combined total of all other raptors. The peak periods of predation were in March and April, when adult kestrels were settling into territories, and in July and August, when a mix of adults and juveniles were recorded as prey items. Furthermore, goshawks, as well as removing the spring breeding population, were also targeting immigrant birds, mostly before they could breed, and this sump effect must have had serious implications on kestrel breeding numbers. The greatest impact was when the kestrel population was at its lowest point, pre-breeding in March and April. The analysis indicated that goshawks killed an average 5.7 kestrels per goshawk home range per breeding season, a huge toll.

*A plucked and half-eaten cock kestrel on a goshawk plucking post*

The work of Brian Little and his team who monitored the kestrels in that area on the back of their merlin work showed around 100 nesting territories in the 1960–1990 period. This was an unplanted sheepwalk, an area of 750 square kilometres, mostly molinia (purple moor grass) and some heather or newly-planted trees. From ringing over 100 kestrels per year, the numbers dropped dramatically until they became very rare as the goshawk colonised. The sheer scale of the decline was staggering: kestrels were 'target practice for goshawks!' as Brian so aptly put it.

From the 1960s to the mid 1980s, Brian Little and his team found 27–30 kestrel nests each year in the 155,000 acres of forest, a total of 164 individual nesting territories. Most were in a variety of sizes of crags, then additionally in crow's nests as the trees matured. The decline began in 1985 and by 2010 only three pairs were recorded breeding, all of them round the edge. The loss of hunting ground as the forest matured, along with the emerging healthy populations of goshawks and peregrines, have taken their toll. An intriguing knock-on effect of the goshawk's feeding on crows is the reduced availability of crow's nests for the kestrel to use. According to data from Brian Little, one of the 2010 kestrel pairs nested in a hole in the gable end of a ruin which had been used since the 1980s.

The level of predation obviously varies across the country and data from northeast Scotland, where probably around 70 pairs of goshawks breed, indicated that the kestrel does not feature highly in the prey taken. Similarly, Malcolm Henderson, working in the Scottish Borders, only finds 1–2 kestrels plucked each year. Data from 2000–2009 in the northeast (Mick Marquiss) includes 2,663 prey items, mostly from 32 sites. There are only 17 kestrels recorded so at 0.64% of the diet, the kestrel seems insignificant to the goshawk population. Kestrels were taken in only seven of the 32 sites.

*Katy Freeman with a trapped juvenile goshawk. Note the incredible size of this raptor*

Of the 17 kestrels taken, 12 were adults or at least full-grown birds and five were dependent juveniles. Of those adults that were sexed, six were males and one was a female. Interestingly, only two kestrels were recorded outside the breeding season (September–February) and most (12 out of 15) were taken in the latter part of the season. Mick concluded that the kestrel was taken regularly in the northeast but not as often as elsewhere, for example in the Border Forest. They were most frequently taken in July and August when the goshawks had fledged young on site. The scale of the predation can be extreme as clearly illustrated in a note I received from Ian Newton on the subject. The location was in Dumfriesshire in 1989.

> It was on 8 July and the four young goshawks were on the wing. Kills were scattered in a wide area round the site, and I counted 22 lots of kestrel feathers that looked to me like separate kills, obviously taken fairly recently. From the flight feathers I put two down as definite adults and the rest as juveniles (many of the latter still had sheaths at the base of the flight feathers).

Ian did state that it was a good area for kestrels with plenty of surrounding sheepwalk for hunting, and that it was also a good year for kestrels in terms of numbers. However, the high proportion of kestrels found in the prey remains exceptional.

Dave Anderson also commented on an interesting feature: although the majority of adults were plucked and eaten near the goshawk's nests, a few were decapitated and left to rot on top of upturned root plates. Later in the breeding cycle a number of family groups of kestrels in the Kielder Forest appeared using restock sites but were 'quickly mopped up' and Dave has seen as many as six individuals left on the root plates, killed but not eaten. On occasion, the remains of family groups were found, identified by rings on the legs and left on nests used by fledged goshawks as feeding points. The untouched bodies were normally found in the latter part of the breeding season when there was an abundance of food.

Kestrels are highly vulnerable, as hovering in open country makes them both conspicuous and an easy target. Goshawks are not the only larger predator that takes advantage of this. In my study areas I have occasionally seen plucked kestrels at peregrine sites and several of the local Raptor Study Groups have recorded similar findings over the years. Golden eagles, too, are not averse to picking off the odd kestrel and David Dick, Duncan Orr-Ewing and Patrick Stirling-Aird have all found the remains of young kestrels on eyries. Pity help the already beleaguered kestrel if the eagle owl *Bubo bubo* becomes an established breeding bird in Scotland.

Compared to other raptor species such as the hen harrier and peregrine falcon, human predation is not a major factor with the kestrel, although it does occasionally rear its ugly head. One incident in 1992 still stirs warm feelings as, against the odds, the egg thieves were thwarted. The start of the season had been dreadful, with low temperatures, wind and rain. By the end of the second week of May, it looked like the disastrous 1986 season would have a rival. Only 12 out of 35 territories checked were occupied and only four clutches recorded. As soon as the weather changed, the transformation was almost instantaneous as 14 more pairs started their cycle.

One of the pairs laid a clutch of four eggs in a hole in the masonry of a cottage gable end on the edge of a conifer forest. The site had been used for many years but unfortunately the new extraction road ran past the ruin, making the site vulnerable. It was actually possible to look into the nest cavity from the road and see the clutch with the naked eye. My diary tells what happened next:

21 June 1991

The intent was to photograph the Gable End pair which often fail to take the cycle to its full term because of the exposed location. In the last ten years, five breeding attempts have failed due mainly to young being stolen. The drive in was unusually bereft of short-eared owls, black grouse, harriers or even kestrels and we had to content ourselves with pipits, skylarks and curlews. Arriving at the site, the buoyant air was replaced with resignation as no bird left the nest hole and, even from the road, I could see that two eggs were missing and the other two were pushed to the back of the cavity. Close inspection revealed recently-trodden grass round the building and an old gate which had been used as a climbing aid.

The eggs were stone cold, which was incredibly frustrating as they had been due to hatch the very next day. I'd already caught the hen a couple of weeks previously and had an accurate first egg laying date. Just to make absolutely certain of the failure we withdrew to a vantage point half a mile away and watched for an hour. The only action came from two pairs of whinchats which were disputing territory among the emerging conifers.

Being so close to the hatching the hen kestrel would have been very attentive to the clutch so sadly we conceded that the pair had deserted. The disturbance had happened very recently, the evidence of the newly-trampled grass was ample proof, so on impulse we decided to take the eggs and try our luck with the Park's incubator. The stone cold eggs were removed and placed next to skin – Deirdre's, not mine – and gradually on the journey back to the Park they began to regain some heat. The aviary at Culzean had just undergone renovation and fortuitously a new incubator had been purchased. The bad news was that it wasn't set up, lacking even a plug. While the eggs hopefully progressed close to Deirdre, I wired the incubator and Deirdre absorbed the instruction manual. We decided that, as the chances were so slim, we'd just put the eggs in at the recommended general temperature of 39°C and live in hope.

Incredibly, plaintive weak cheeping was heard from one of the eggs the next morning and just after eight o'clock a small crack appeared in the shell. Who would have believed it? Maybe we could salvage something after all. This is what happened:

22 June

0800

Eggs moving gently and the first vestige of a crack noted in one egg. The plaintive cheeping continued all day.

Day 1, 23 June

0820

The crack on top of one of the eggs had noticeably widened, both "eggs" were very vocal and movement in the cracked egg was continuous.

0845

The crack had extended round the top third of the egg as if someone had tapped it all the way round. Things were moving fast.

0850

It all happened so suddenly. One minute the egg was there, the next a wet and bedraggled pinkish body, eyes completely dwarfing the head, orange feet tucked into the body and a prominent egg tooth. Absolute elation in the office.

1200

Chick had dried out completely and was calling for food, its head thrust upwards in a begging posture flashing a brilliant red/orange gape. Very gently tiny morsels of raw meat were put in the beak. Absolutely no problem, it took three then collapsed into a heap and slept. Already it had passed a dropping and another followed after its first feed. The other egg was still very noisy and moving about a lot. A crack had appeared.

The policy of feeding little and often was employed with considerable success. The office became a mecca for all the staff as the word spread. The chick was very mobile and noisy too.

1415

Another feed, chick much more active than I would have guessed at such an early stage.

2050

Second egg very active, rolling around, and a regular 'tap tap' indicated that the chick was working hard. Last feed for the first bird and I suspect that it won't be long before both are hatched.

Day 2, 24 June

0820

Second chick had hatched and was drying out nicely. It must have hatched a couple of hours ago. The noise level had increased perceptibly. Same pattern, a few morsels of meat then the collapse and sleep. Close comfort with each other. Fed the new chick after an hour. Took two small morsels then collapsed in a heap with the effort. Both birds the centre of attention. Fed regularly throughout the day and amazingly, when the younger sibling had dried, out the size differential had shrunk considerably.

The thought of them becoming imprinted or consigned to captivity does not appeal, so a determined effort will be made to find a compatible brood for fostering. The problem lies in the lack of options at this late time, even in a late season. Possibilities are the Forestry Commission site, the ICI factory at Ardeer, where a pair has laid in an incredibly difficult site to access (a pipe high in a disused building with a rusty old filter fan between us and the nest), or the Magpie Wood. My money would be on the last.

Day 3, 25 June

First effort to locate a foster site. One possibility is in the high sitka in the Rock study area. A cuckoo was being mobbed by pipits, but still persisted in calling, as we crossed into the wood, and young rabbits scattered into cover. It was ominously quiet at the site, the highest climb on the circuit. My estimate was 60 feet, Deirdre's 50 – but she wasn't climbing. Sixty feet later and I was staring into an empty nest. No sign of hatching and no indication of when the bird had deserted. One down. Two other pairs had chicks ready for ringing, so we moved quickly on to the Kestrel Wood. As we rounded the wood the hen kestrel flew up from a grassy knoll next to the woodland edge and landed on the nest tree. If the noise was anything to go on the chicks were doing well. We moved cautiously forward until we were within 30 metres and were able to stand and watch the whole operation. Who needs a hide?

She was standing at the back of the nest, tail braced upwards against the trunk, so intent on feeding her offspring that we continued to go unnoticed. The young were begging furiously, wings thrashing and heads thrust forward. Session over, she moved adroitly past the nestlings, ran along a branch then launched herself out over the wood. She headed out over the hill, still oblivious to the intruders.

The four young got more than they bargained for as dessert. I was halfway through the ringing when the hen at last picked us up and circled anxiously in a wide arc. The nest is holding up well but this is its last productive year. The long-eared owl's nest in the old kestrel box was checked and out came an adult, still on two eggs – on 24 June!

Next step was the new nest box in the forestry ground – unit 3 – and this time Deirdre did climb the tree. All five young had hatched and were ringed amid hordes of spiteful midges. The interesting point was that the young were not as well developed as the previous brood despite having hatched several days earlier. The extra mouth to feed must be making a difference even in this good weather. So far, no rain for seven weeks and the point has been reached at the Kestrel Wood Farm that the farmer is pumping water from a stream and transporting it round the farm in a bowser.

Still, the season is coming together. Nine kestrels ringed tonight and seven last night. One of the sites visited last night with Duncan Cameron was in an upland cleugh.

The kestrels had forsaken their normal ledge site for a huge raven's stick platform on top of a mature rowan tree. Although the tree was easy to climb, catching the young was no mean feat as the depth of the massive structure was at least four feet and as it was at the topmost section of the tree, my arms were just too short. Eventually, legs were caught and three young were recorded for posterity. The midges were horrendous again and everything was done at pace.

Day 4, 26 June
Although the younger bird is definitely catching up, the size difference is still noticeable and when food is proffered there are already signs of sibling rivalry, the older chick grabbing at the younger bird's food. However, when feeding is over they quickly settle down to rest together. Both birds' eyes are open and they respond to fingers snapping, the signal that food is served.

The quest for a suitable brood continued, the net widening to the Waterhead study area. Both adults were in the air above the Ram Wood, which was a bit out of character so I revised my timetable and walked in to investigate. Magpie chatter and chaffinch alarm greeted my entry into the wood. I needn't have worried as the five young were all well but, unfortunately, just too far ahead of our two. Fostering into a brood of five would not be advisable anyway as it would put far too much pressure on the adults.

The Magpie Wood was always the front runner, so it came as a great relief to see the hen kestrel vacate the nest box. Four young were huddled in the scrape and, although they were a couple of days advanced, a good feeding programme should enable the orphans to catch up.

Last in line was the Dipper Wood. This vocal pair were ideal for recording so, tape deck in hand, I forced my way through the young conifer plantation, past a whitethroat and a lesser redpoll in full song. Hardly had I reached the wood when in she came, screaming, closely followed by her mate. I climbed the tree very carefully, mindful of the chances of a premature explosion of first flights. Three were still in the nest and one out on a branch so I descended quickly. I then spent the next two hours in a search along the tree line which stretched endlessly into the distance, just in case a second pair was present. I found only a tawny owl, disturbed as it roosted at the woodland edge.

Back home I telephoned Eddie Miller and he reported two chicks hatched in the pipe, an ideal size but logistically very difficult as it would be impossible to guarantee getting the young into the scrape – great potential for an accident and an unrecoverable situation. However, a last resort if the Magpie Wood fails.

## Day 5, 27 June

The younger chick is giving some cause for concern as it is not feeding so readily, but it is still taking enough to keep itself going. Both chicks are now in a hospital cage rather than the incubator and the temperature is being gradually reduced in preparation for farming them out into a much more hostile environment.

## Day 6, 28 June

Thankfully, the younger chick has revived and is looking good. Deirdre did the bulk of the feeding and the smaller bird has almost caught up.

## Days 7 and 8, 29 and 30 June

Progress is excellent, both birds feeding well, sleeping well and preening regularly. The glass on the front of the hospital cage, the 'edge of the nest', is becoming splattered with droppings as they fire out of their chosen resting place.

## Day 9, July 1

We drove up to the Magpie Wood and parked the car at the usual spot. It was time for a final feeding session to give both birds a good start. They fed eagerly, unconcerned at the unfamiliar location and unaffected by the journey. We packed as much as we could into the gapes until finally they couldn't and wouldn't take any more. They were then placed in a bag and carried to the base of the tree. The relief was audible as the hen left the nest box and we both climbed the tree. All the feeding had not been in vain as the orphans had almost caught up on the four nestlings. They were put into the scrape and immediately huddled close to the pack, the smallest burrowing into the middle. Within seconds, the integration was complete, no adverse reaction from incomers or residents, just a heap of beaks and pot bellies. We'd done our bit: now it was up to the kestrels.

## 20 July

The moment of truth. It's now 19 days since the two young kestrels were fostered and, in the interim, I have fitted in a family holiday in Orkney – for the second year in succession. The island kestrels have not fared very well and of the three ground nesters only one has managed to raise young. Hen harriers have suffered too, but the merlin figures were the best for years and Keith and I went out with Eric Meek ringing broods. Over 40 young were ringed in the season, a very healthy sign.

Back to the Magpie territory, but despite the apprehension I positively carried the camera bag as well as the rings. It was very quiet in the wood but the ground under the nest box was white and a couple of heads peered down then shuffled back into cover. The climb was incredible as the branches were literally plastered with droppings and down clung to the sitka needles.

Finally, my head came level with the box and triggered the explosion. Two brown streaks flashed past my left ear and bounced down the branches to where Deirdre waited as back stop. Another clipped my right ear as it made its bid to avoid becoming a statistic. It landed a couple of metres away, wings outstretched as it clung to a bushy branch. Not daring to move quickly, I stretched out, caught it and popped in into the bag. The moment of truth had arrived and I peered into the recess of the box. Three more heads, fantastic, all six had survived and were in great condition. I shouted the news down to Deirdre, who was by this time scuffling under the spruce branches trying to catch 'Mansell' whose elusive skills and cornering ability managed to outmanoeuvre her for a couple of minutes. A poor decision eventually trapped it as refuge was sought under a root plate. Even so, Deirdre came up smelling sour as sheep had also been using the spot.

*Cock kestrel at the Gable End nest site*

*The moment of hatching. Note the regular cut made using the egg tooth*

*Just hatched and ready to dry out*        *One hatched in the incubator and one to go*

*No problems at feeding time as both birds took readily to the prepared meat*

Poor light dictated that the ringing and photography needed to be done out on the open hill and the celebrities were well and truly recorded on celluloid. My jacket was also photographed as it had undergone a complete colour transformation from green to white because of the whitewash on the trunk and branches.

*Above: Climbing trees at this stage in the cycle can be messy*

*Right: Whitewash, one of the downsides of the work*

All the birds were in good condition, a tribute to the hunting prowess of the adults which, up to this point, had not put in an appearance. Both birds were possibly out on the hill in search of more prey.

Ringing and photography over, the process of repatriation into the nest box was a slow one. Each bird was carefully placed into the cavity, as we tried in vain to avoid the nasty jabs from the others while preventing escape bids. At last they were all lined up, a formidable squad facing outwards at the back of the box. Now 29 days old they still had several more days to go before their first flight and another visit would be needed. It's always a shorter journey home after a successful operation.

Another rescue mission which I heard of happened in Northumberland in 1978. Brian Little, Eric Meek and Brian Etheridge were checking kestrel nests on 17 May when they found a waterlogged and deserted nest with four eggs in an old exposed eagle site. No birds were present but a fresh scrape in a more sheltered ledge on the north end of the crag indicated that the pair were probably going to re-lay. Down feathers at the side of the scrape and nibbled willow herb stems were positive pointers.

As the four eggs were obviously fresh they were dried and moved into the alternative site, more in hope than expectation. On 28 May a second visit was made and a male kestrel came off eight eggs: there was no way of telling by looking which was from the first or second batches. So far, so good.

Remarkably, on 25 June, seven nestlings were found in the nest but as there was no sign of the eighth egg, presumably all eight had hatched and one had subsequently perished. At a second territory a few kilometres away, another kestrel pair had re-laid after losing its clutch in the same bad spell of weather and three nestlings had hatched. As they were roughly the same age, and to give the chicks a better chance of surviving, two of the smallest young from the seven were fostered onto the second pair, leaving two broods of five. All ten birds were later ringed and fledged successfully.

Ever since I read the late Eddie Balfour's account of ground nesting kestrels in Orkney (Balfour 1955) I had wanted to see one of these sites for myself and the opportunity came in

*All six safely ringed*

*Six out of six, the fostered birds indistinguishable from the original brood*

*Early photograph of a ground-nesting kestrel on Orkney*

52 1991. No one believed that the family holiday was motivated by anything but kestrels, despite my protestations of innocence.

So one afternoon, six days into the holiday – a long time to wait – Keith and I set out in the capable hands of Eric Meek, the RSPB representative on Orkney, to visit one or two raptor sites. It was a changeable day, the sun burning out the mist in certain parts of the island while banks of fresh all-enveloping pea soup drifted into other areas. Embarrassingly, I'd not yet laid eyes upon a kestrel. Today, things would be different.

Moving on to high ground, the car was parked at the edge of a spur of heath moorland and immediately a short-eared owl was spotted hunting along the roadside. Traversing the half mile or so to the first hen harrier site was a new experience as the spongy, unpredictable mix of greater woodrush and heather continually threw us off line. The Orcadians have a name for this terrain: treeless woodland. We passed a flattened platform in the rushes, used as a roosting spot by one of the adults.

A female hen harrier came into view, yikkering in an agitated manner as we closed in on the nest site. From a visit the previous week, Eric knew that two of the young, both males, had left the nest, but the hope was that the slower-developing female chick would still be there and could be wing-tagged. She was already ringed. The smaller cock birds mature more quickly and leave the nest much earlier than the hens.

Suddenly one juvenile, obviously well-fledged, closely followed by a second, flew strongly out of the nest area and out onto the hill. We moved in warily but the young female was still nest-bound and merely retreated to the back of the platform. She was easily gathered up by Eric who proceeded to put a coloured tag on each wing – blue on the right, to signify Orkney-bred, red and yellow on the left to reflect year and sex. In other parts of the country

*Wing-tagged hen harrier chick*

different colour coding is used and the scheme's aim is to shed more light on the dispersal and movement of these heavily-persecuted birds. Orkney is one of the main strongholds in Britain of this beautiful bird of prey, supporting roughly 70 females and just over 20 males.

All through the operation, while the tags had been pinned to the thin membrane near the main wing bone, the bird had behaved with little aggression and, despite the adult female circling above, had never uttered a sound. She was returned to the nest and photographed.

No sooner had we moved away than a hen kestrel flew over, crossing the traffic of Arctic and great skuas. We hoped that the maxim of 'Once you've seen one, you see a lot' would apply. Barely a quarter of a mile over the hillside was a short-eared owl's nest – and what a beauty it was. The heather formed a perfect semi-circle to frame the three two-and-a-half week old owlets which remained absolutely motionless, peering with their sad eyes up at the intruders. There was no sign of the adults this time as the three were ringed, weighed and measured before returning to their vigil among the moulted feathers, pipits' feathers and pellets. Again the islands boast a very healthy population – about 50 pairs – of this bird, which is the only owl species to breed there.

Another drive, this time into a lovely little glen with the air almost of a time capsule with its track up to the croft, heather hillsides and old peat workings. A family of stonechats broke the monotony of meadow pipits as we carried a hide up to the second harrier site of the day. Eric was putting in the first stage of the hide about 40 metres from the nest site. Once the hide was erected, the nest was checked and off she came, leaving two bemused ten-day old chicks in a very open situation. Both birds had bulging crops and the fresh remains of an adult rat lay at the edge of the platform. The female held back about 30 metres and was joined by her mate who flew around calling, before landing on a banking, giving us superb views of what must be one of the most striking of our raptors. We left immediately and she was in at the site before we had crossed the first ridge. Although it was a late brood, it had every chance of a successful outcome, given that sort of attention and only two mouths to feed.

Before we set out for the kestrel site we had the bonus of a cup of tea and home-made Orkney shortbread from the old woman at the croft. On such a clammy day the refreshment was most welcome, as was the hospitality. Eric kept her fully informed as to the progress of the breeding attempt. On the drive over to the kestrel site we managed to photograph a snipe on a fence post. Photography on Orkney is a most frustrating pastime, as only a few of the hundreds of attempts at oystercatchers and curlews ever turn out well.

The car stopped and I could see the huge bank of heather on the hillside, more typically merlin territory, where Eric had ringed four out of five young a week ago. He was not sure whether the nest would have survived or if the young would still be in the nest.

After a chat with the farmer, who assured us that the power to the electric fence was off, we crossed the fields and were soon ploughing through deep meadow which, thankfully, was dry. The same could not be said of the deep cut banks of the main drainage channel, though, and although Eric and I managed to leap over, Keith had the misfortune to take off from an unsafe edge and dive headlong into the opposite bank, before slowly sinking, to our amusement, into the stream. It was thigh-high heather from then on as the incline rose sharply.

Halfway up and the telltale down feathers clung to the tips of the heather, the only sign of kestrels in the sea of ling. The site itself was not quite as I'd imagined it: simply a hole in the heather bank, completely enclosed by mature heather stems, the kestrels dropping directly in. It was very reminiscent of merlin sites I'd seen in the past.

The smell was there, the whitewash and the nest litter, but not the kestrel chicks. Suddenly, scuttling noises could be heard in different parts of the labyrinth and the search was on. Three struggling, almost fully-grown youngsters, all ringed, were extracted from their hiding places, and a fourth, the unringed runt which was doing very well, was eventually located, playing at ostriches well off the actual site boundary. A telltale movement of heather even further out gave the game away and the final chick was reunited with its siblings.

Now came the shuffling around of young – there are never enough hands when the birds are this age – as the runt was ringed and the rest of the chicks weighed and measured. Keith, once again, was the only casualty as a copious direct hit was scored to his 'Scotland' shellsuit jacket from a very excited chick's rear end. It was clearly not his day. Job done and photographs taken, the young were replaced fleetingly onto the original scrape before scattering again in all directions. Both adults must have been out hunting as there had been no response to the excited calling of the young during the visit. By the time we'd gone 20 metres, the site had once more become anonymous.

Extensive fieldwork by Eric, wardens and other raptor enthusiasts on Orkney had only recorded four pairs nesting on the ground that year, a far cry from the heady days of the 1950s and 1960s when ground nesting was at its peak. At least nineteen territories were known at that time but over the last four decades a steady decline of this type of nest site has been seen.

Ground nesting on the Orkney Isles is common among many species and is indeed a necessity in an environment where tree sites are at a premium. Critically, too, there is a dearth

*Eric and Keith at the ground-nest site on the heather-clad slope*

*Brood of four eventually found scattered in deep cover round the nest*

of ground predators, particularly of foxes, stoats and weasels, although the feral cat does pose a threat. On Papa Westray, I had first-hand experience of an individual in action. Waking at sunrise, I was admiring the beauty of the island when a cat appeared in front of the window carrying a newly-caught Arctic tern in its mouth.

Wood pigeons and hooded crows have taken to using heathery sites alongside the more traditional inhabitants such as the merlin, hen harrier and red grouse. Eric pointed out a copse of stunted willow which had hosted a breeding attempt by a sparrowhawk that year, the nest being only a few feet off the ground.

Interpretation of the kestrel's position is not easy. Ground nests were generally quite successful, and food stocks, including the abundant Orkney vole, peculiar to the islands, still sustained healthy numbers of short-eared owls and hen harriers in the early 1990s. Potential nest sites abound on buildings – a pair regularly breed in the tower of St Magnus' Cathedral in Kirkwall – cliff faces, in quarries and, of course, on the ground. Persecution is negligible.

Yet the kestrel is very definitely on the decline and is by no means the most common raptor. In 1991, the number of territories occupied by the kestrel was down to around 20, another tantalizing mystery which will no doubt tax the minds of fieldworkers in the future. Similarly, where are all the buzzards which might be expected on Orkney, teeming as it does with their main prey, the rabbit? It is an extremely rare breeding raptor on mainland Orkney where conditions would again seem to be ideal.

Still, the pilgrimage had been well worth the effort, though two sightings of adult kestrels in two weeks were hardly enough to sustain me.

On a more recent holiday on Orkney, I visited the Tomb of the Eagles on South Ronaldsay, an exciting site where Neolithic remains are well preserved. The tribal sub-group which lived in this area and practiced excarnation had as its totem the white-tailed sea eagle and these birds featured prominently in rituals connected to death. The totem skulls and talons were buried with the dead, often with as much ceremony as if they belonged to a human being. Smaller numbers of bones of short-eared owl, goshawk and kestrel were also found at the site (Hedges 1984). Dating from around 5,000 years ago, this must be the earliest record of kestrels.

*Sea eagle claws recovered from the Tomb of the Eagles*

Another island ploy involved a double trip to the nearby Isle of Bute in 1993. The season was turning out quite badly as continuous heavy rain, the coldest May Day on record, severe winds and snow above 200 metres decimated the kestrel breeding attempts. The only good news came from Bute, where Ian Hopkins had seen a leucistic hen kestrel at a known territory and, on investigating further, had found a clutch of five eggs (leucistic means a pale form of albinism where the pigments are lost from the feathers but not from the rest of the body).

Thoughts immediately turned to the two birds I had ringed in 1990 which had moulted into almost-white birds. Could one of them have survived and be breeding on Bute? I made arrangements to visit the pair once the monsoon abated, although Ian was fairly certain that she wasn't ringed.

The widely-anticipated visit to Bute turned into another family outing, encouraged by a flat calm Firth of Clyde and the prospect of an enjoyable ferry crossing. Ian, guide and chauffeur for the day, met us at the terminal at Rothesay and all the gear was transferred into the green

*Two leucistic and one normal-plumaged youngster in the brood of three*

camper. Ian has been involved in the Raptor Study Group since its inception in 1982 and he was one of the first roving RSPB wardens in southwest Scotland in the early 1970s.

It really was an exceptional early June day and the fact that Ian was a key-holder to the forest saved a long hot haul up into the hills. We viewed the crag from the car then dropped Rosie off to act as the lookout, just in case the hen came off the nest prematurely. The rest of the troops crossed the forest drains until we were above the cliff. It was a classic old raven eyrie with an overhang, but thankfully the pair had chosen to breed on a reasonably accessible ledge fronted by scrub oak. I inched forward until I was on the edge and there she was, a sandy, fawn face staring back at me as she covered her clutch of eggs. I managed one photograph before she exited through a well-worn gap in the oak branches, exposing five eggs.

She was so obvious in flight: pale, like a barn owl, against the early green of the young sitka. I roped off and scrambled down to collect three priceless feathers, which could be of value in the future if more leucistic birds are found and DNA genetic fingerprinting can be used to determine family links. The eggs were quite unusual, being more elongated and pointed than normal and, on checking, two did not show signs of embryo development.

The trap was set and we were able to cover the area from the relative luxury of the van. She came in very quickly, hovered over the site for a few minutes, showing dark patches on the wings, then dropped into the trap. The adrenalin flow was unbelievable: suddenly something really positive had happened this season.

We crossed the young conifer plantation at the double and the fleeting disappointment at an unringed bird was quickly dispelled as she was ringed, weighed and photographed. Her feathers were in good condition but her weight, at 245 grams, was well below average. She was in moult, as was to be expected of an incubating hen, but the interesting point was that the dark patches were caused by several darker primary and secondary feathers on both wings. The bird was definitely leucistic.

*The adult leucistic hen trapped on Bute*

Time, as usual, was not on our side and she was quickly released. Once more she did the grand tour then quickly returned to her eggs as we made our way back to the van. We were ecstatic.

The next three weeks were spent checking out the failures or ringing the broods. A second trip was made to Bute to see the three chicks which did hatch, but, unlike their parent, they showed normal plumage coloration. All three were ringed and fledged successfully.

# 3

# Peaks and gecko blasters

1997 was a very significant year for kestrels in south Ayrshire, being the most productive for breeding pairs since I began monitoring. It was also my 25th consecutive year of kestrel work, a personal milestone which I could not have contemplated back in the early 1970s. And, just to put the icing on the cake, a trip to the Seychelles and Mauritius provided a wonderful opportunity to see at first hand two of the rarer kestrels of the world.

The build-up to the season started well with visits in January to several nesting territories to check nest boxes and erect a few more. There was little expectation of seeing kestrels in the upland study areas due to the icy conditions. On lower ground, bramblings fed on the beech mast crushed by passing cars while at Culzean, the place to be was in the walled garden where blackbirds and mistle thrushes competed with a small colourful band of invading waxwings for the equally colourful crab apples. The chance of an encounter with a kestrel is much greater on the lower ground where nesting territories can often support individuals and even pairs throughout the winter. The birds keep in regular touch with the core nest sites, especially during the warm sunny spells, and displays and nest inspections can occur at any time.

February was a complete wipe-out as gales and horizontal rain meant that fieldwork was out of the question other than at low elevations. By contrast, March and April, though still cold, were reasonably dry months and early indications were that vole numbers were heading for a cyclic peak. As the snow retreated from grassy areas, the labyrinth of surface tunnels was exposed and on one occasion, while inspecting a box in a forestry plantation, the ground below me seemed alive with voles.

It was no great surprise when a kestrel egg was found in a nest box on 27 March, the earliest date recorded until now in the study area. It ran true to form: despite regular changeover of breeding adults, this particular nesting territory, the Heron Wood, invariably hosted the pair of kestrels which laid the earliest clutches. To the human eye, though, this territory had no special features and was no different in composition or structure from any others in the surrounding area.

Not all the birds had fared well in the late winter months and a female was found dead at the Dam site, tucked in behind the old hide which I'd used in the past. A check on the ring

*Labyrinths of runs in vole peak years*

*Keith with lively brood of seven from the Dam territory*

number revealed that she had been caught in the same territory as a first-year breeder in 1991 so she had done extremely well to reach the ripe old age of seven. Small falcons such as the kestrel have a rapid population turnover and rely upon the early maturity of birds and large clutch sizes to compensate for a heavy mortality of juveniles (60%) in their first winter (Cavé 1968 and Riddle 1992).

From this point on, the season was all about statistical records. Nearly all kestrel hens begin laying in April and this is usually a good marker as early breeders tend to lay large clutches and rear most young, and these young have a better chance of surviving their first winter than do later fledglings. The net result was an average clutch size of 5.8 eggs for the breeding pairs, including 18 sixes and one seven. Eighty per cent of eggs hatched and brood survival was at an all time high at 95%. Hens which were trapped as part of an ongoing pro-gramme to check adult turnover were all at the top range of body weights, between 282 and 306 grams. The broods were well fed as the weather and vole numbers held up throughout May and June.

The analysis of figures at the end of the season revealed very high productivity, an average of four young fledging per breeding pair. It was no surprise that the most productive pair bred at the Dam, a nesting territory which had consistently housed successful pairs in good and bad years. The alternative site on a cliff face was used this year and on the first foray over the edge I found a clutch of six. So inconvenient was it to get to the cramped ledge that I used binoculars on my next visit, pinpointing the six heads from the safety of the clifftop. Imagine my surprise when seven feisty bundles were retrieved from behind the heather at ringing time – yet another small record. One clutch of eight eggs and a couple of sevens had been recorded in the past but none of the birds had managed to rear all the progeny which hatched. It took all Keith's wits to keep the seven in place while I photographed them.

This impressive response to ideal feeding conditions and food availability was not matched by all the avian predators. Long-eared owls do occasionally breed in the study area and I'm delighted if I can locate even one pair. Their prey items include 80% or more small mammals, of which half are field voles. It was a measure of the vole peak in 1997 that no fewer than six pairs attempted to breed, more than the total for the past ten years. Sadly, they had a poor success rate.

One pair which used a kestrel box in a shelter belt of sitka spruce laid a clutch of four eggs, ranging in size from one of normal dimensions to a blackbird-sized one for the smallest. This possibly indicated an inexperienced first-year hen laying for the first time. Two pairs failed in almost identical circumstances, three young at about the ten week stage being found dead on the ground below the nests with no visible signs of predation. Their crops were empty which could indicate that the parents had deserted or been predated. Work in the 1970s, further south in Eskdalemuir, showed that although the proportion of pairs attempting to breed was highest in years of vole abundance, the percentage of hatched young which fledged was highest when vole numbers were scarce. The implication was that in poor years only 'better quality' pairs bred, while in good years birds which were possibly not in prime condition would also attempt to breed.

*Long-eared owlets in old crow's nest*

*Clutch of long-eared owl eggs showing huge variation in size*

I did once find a young long-eared owl in very poor condition, its eyes caked over with nest debris, blinding it completely. Back home we bathed it for over an hour with warm water till eventually all the muck was removed. Nicknamed Scruff, we fed it for several days to build up its strength as it had obviously been unattended on the woodland floor for a time and was very lightweight. My daughter Gael was particularly attached to it and came with me when it was released back into the same wood where the rest of its family were still hanging around.

Geoff Shaw also experienced a year to remember with the barn owl. The first egg was laid on 21 March and laying continued into August resulting in young fledging as late as November. Clutch sizes averaged out at over six eggs per pair and, like the kestrel, most successful pairs reared at least six young. Four pairs even double-brooded, something which has not been recorded with the European kestrel which sticks very rigidly to a single-brood strategy.

Barn owls do have the capability to respond rapidly to the vole cycle, enabling them to recover from poor years when output is poor and birds may not even breed. The four double-brooded pairs, for example, reared 39 chicks between them, more than the 34 chicks produced from the total sampled population in 1996. In 1995, the position had been even worse when more than 30 pairs were lost from the sample population.

The combined data relating to productivity and vole cycles illustrates essential differences between the two species. While both birds benefit in years when vole numbers are high, barn owl productivity drops dramatically when the voles crash and can take several years to recover. The reason is that the barn owl is unable to switch to other food sources as easily as the kestrel, which has much more catholic tastes. By taking alternatives such as juvenile starlings, pipits and skylarks, the kestrel continues to produce young, albeit at a reduced rate.

On 2 October, the day Rosie and I flew out to the Seychelles and Mauritius, Geoff ringed four broods of barn owls while two other pairs still had very small young. My fieldwork with the kestrel had been over for two months.

Although the three-week trip to the Seychelles and Mauritius was to be a holiday, it has to be admitted that there was a very strong kestrel agenda. Both these groups of Indian Ocean islands support endemic populations of kestrels and for years I'd promised myself a visit to see them at close quarters. Before the trip I did my homework, reading up as much as possible on the islands and their fauna and making contact with an old friend in the Seychelles and a kestrel acquaintance in Mauritius, both of whom were to prove invaluable. The timing of the visit was also critical, as we were leaving autumn in the northern hemisphere to enjoy the spring south of the equator, and the beginning of the kestrels' breeding cycle.

First port of call was the Seychelles, a group of 115 islands covering a staggering 152,000 square miles of Indian Ocean yet, remarkably, with a land mass of only 175 square miles. We used the main island Mahé as a base and from there visited Praslin and Cousin.

First impressions were of an idyllic setting for a holiday but the dense vegetation from sea level to summits seemed daunting from a kestrel-viewing perspective. This was borne out when after the first four days we'd seen only three individuals: one close up, sitting on a wire near the hotel, one flying across the road and a third in the capital Victoria. The first bird was the only one which allowed decent observation as it took off, grabbed a gecko from the trunk of a tree and, returning to another perch, proceeded to eat it. The wing beats in flight were very rapid compared with the European kestrel.

PEAKS AND GECKO BLASTERS

*Secondary vegetation on Mahé. Little of the primary forestry habitat remains*

Open space was at a premium on the island and all three birds were seen in relatively built-up areas where the vegetation was less suffocating. Despite knowing what to expect from textbook descriptions, it was still a surprise to realize that this colourful kestrel (*Falco araea*) is the same size as our blackbird and weighs only 80–90 grams. The diagnostic field marks are chestnut wings with black spots, a dark crown and unmarked underparts. Unfortunately we had little opportunity to admire the bird as it was extremely difficult to spot, especially from a car. Such was the condition of the road verges that you took your eye off the road at your peril.

The history of the kestrel in the Seychelles is fascinating as it follows in part the usual trend of decline in small island populations, but then recovers to a relatively stable level. From being 'totally common' (Newton 1867), the species had declined to fewer than 30 birds on the main island Mahé by the mid 1960s and was considered to be critically endangered and close to extinction (Gaymer *et al.* 1969).

The usual suspects were implicated in the demise: the destruction of the prime natural habitat, persecution, pesticides and the introduction of non-native species. The reduction of the natural vegetation for logging, coconut plantations, commercial cinnamon cultivation and agriculture occurred during the 18th and 19th centuries. In the past, the species has been thought to be unlucky and its presence in the vicinity of a settlement was said to indicate an imminent death. On top of these superstitions, its old Creole name was 'manger d' poul' and although it could not kill chickens, the result was widespread persecution.

Potential predators on its eggs and young include the Indian mynah, the green-backed heron, the black rat, feral cats and the barn owl. Ironically, but typical of the situation on the islands, the only endemic species on that list is the heron, the rest having been introduced by man in the last two centuries. The case of the barn owl is a classic example of what can happen when a new species is added to a new environment.

*Green-backed heron, an occasional predator of kestrel young*

The African barn owl was brought to the Seychelles in 1951 and 1952 in an attempt to control the rat problems on the islands by natural means. Instead of following the script, the owls developed a taste for the beautiful fairy terns whose pure white plumage makes them an easy target in the dark. The barn owl also competes for nest sites with kestrels and will predate them too. Currently there is a government bounty on the barn owl and numbers seem to be falling. Certainly we did not see one bird during our ten-day stay.

*The introduced barn owls found the fairy terns easy prey*

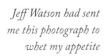

*Jeff Watson had sent me this photograph to whet my appetite*

Up until the 1970s, little was known about the breeding biology of the Seychelles kestrel but between 1975 and 1977 the late Jeff Watson carried out a detailed study of the birds on Mahé. He estimated that the population for the Seychelles was in the region of 150–300 birds so a recovery had occurred. Later work put the population at around 370 pairs on Mahé, Praslin and Silhoutte (Watson 1981 and 1992). By the mid 1980s, the position had further improved with Collar and Stuart (1985) describing the species as being far more numerous and widespread than previously thought. The population seemed relatively stable and the most up-to-date figure from Skerret *et al.* (2001) was around 440 pairs while Gerlach (2008) put the figures on Mahé at 450 pairs and on Silhoutte at 50 pairs. The population is probably between 500 and 550 pairs at present.

This back-from-the-brink story has been further researched by Groombridge *et al.* in a paper published in 2009. They suggest that the Seychelles kestrel endured a recent and severe population crash in the last 150 years which may have approached the severity of the Mauritius kestrel's decline. The genetic data they obtained pinpointed the most severe population bottleneck as having occurred after 1940, a bottleneck being the reduction of a population to a very few individuals with, potentially, a severe loss in genetic diversity. The significance of the recovery is explained in a quote from their paper:

'Together these field records raise the intriguing possibility that the Seychelles kestrel has recovered from a severe population bottleneck relatively unaided by conservation efforts in comparison to the recovery of the Mauritius kestrel (*Falco punctatus*), a closely related oceanic island endemic which was successfully rescued from the brink of extinction by 25 years of intense conservation management'. (Jones *et al.* 1995, Groombridge *et al.* 2001 and 2009).

The only conservation programme in the Seychelles was a small translocation of 13 birds to Praslin in 1977, which had limited success. There are several factors which together have facilitated this incredible recovery, not least that the habitat loss has had much less impact on the Seychelles kestrel than on its Mauritius counterpart. The replacement tree cover on Mahé still sustained the main prey of the kestrel, namely the gecko and lizard population, and 25% of Mahé has been designated as National Park, thus securing habitat suitable for the kestrel and other species.

The use of DDT and other pesticides was not widespread in the Seychelles, limited to small- scale trials to control agricultural pests and to localized spraying. The government has also been proactive in the control of invasive species such as barn owls and rats. Very positive conservation measures have recently been proposed, such as nest protection and awareness in Praslin, an extension of the Marine Seychellois National Park and future translocation possibilities.

Fundamental to all this is the continued monitoring of the population and the public education and awareness campaigns. Nature Seychelles, an environmental conservation organization, has as part of its programme a 'Help Save the Seychelles Kestrel' project which focuses on gaining public participation in saving the kestrel. Predator-proof nest boxes are provided to be placed around schools and other public buildings and high-profile locations. Boxes are even provided for private dwellings and awareness campaigns are promoted through the Wildlife Club of Seychelles.

Due to the relatively small size of the population it is still classed as 'vulnerable' on the IUCN red list evaluated by Birdlife International and listed on Appendix 1 of CITES. Huge progress has been made, however, and I hope that an improved designation will come in the fullness of time.

But back to 1997. As the days progressed and the kestrels remained elusive, we began to suffer nagging doubts that we might never touch base with the bird. We'd ticked off the shy Chinese bittern at the Plantation Club Hotel, the rare magpie robin had been photographed on Cousin, the black parrot's whistle had attracted us to it on Praslin and the fairy tern had been eyeballed on Cousin, brooding its large eggs, incredibly enough, on the bare branches of trees.

We'd even seen the bare-legged scops owl, thanks in no small measure to John Collie, formerly a seasonal ranger at Culzean who had returned to his roots on Mahé and was now director of the Marine Park off that island. In less than hospitable conditions we'd taken a tape recorder up into the mountains late one night to try and lure this shy tiny owl. The population size is said to be 80 pairs but as they are restricted to some of the densest upland areas, no-one had ever, up to that point, found a nest and the owl's diet was virtually unknown. The bird was thought to be extinct from 1906 to 1959 when a local bird enthusiast rediscovered it, causing a sensation in ornithological circles. The slow rhythmic rasping call sounds like a saw on wood, hence its Creole name, 'woodcutter'. The rain did eventually abate and the tape lure did its job calling in two of these diminutive owls, the only owl species found naturally in the Seychelles.

Two days from the end of the stay John called to say that there was possibly a pair of kestrels nesting on St Anne's Island, in one of the old buildings where he worked, and that he would take us over. He had sent me a series of photographs taken on the island including the illustration of one using a washing line as a perch. Unfortunately he had to cancel, much to our disappointment, but we rearranged for the next day. It was to be our last day and the heavens opened monsoon-style, causing great anxiety. John, though, decided to press on and the diary account describes the finale to our stay:

*The secondary forest on St Anne's Island supports a healthy prey population for the kestrels*

12 October 1997

We dreaded another negative call from John but thankfully it never came, so off we went to the rendezvous point at the Marine Charter Company jetty. The route to Victoria was now well known and at the flooded mangrove swamp we took time to photograph a grey heron perched on the crossbar of one goal on the half-submerged football pitch. At

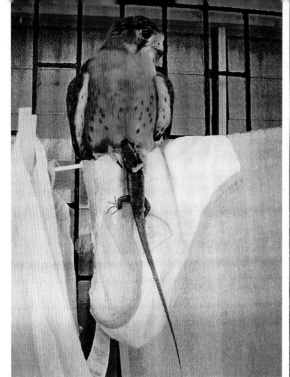

*John Collie had a pair of birds nesting in the Park admin building, using all available perches*

*A bad hair day for the egrets after heavy rain*

68

the harbour the squalls continued but a pair of common sandpipers brought a touch of Scotland to the scene. Ahead was a small island which housed a colony of cattle egrets and grey herons and a constant flow of birds headed in and out of town, probably bound for the food market. As we sailed past the egrets, some of which were on eggs, they hung around miserably crests sagging in the conditions – a real 'bad hair day'.

The 15-minute trip over was bumpy but uneventful and we arrived at John's office drenched. We had coats on but the rain on the outside was matched by the perspiration on the inside. Under the palms, the usual mix of ground and turtle doves pecked away at the vegetation while the background noise was provided by around twenty mynahs. Various sizes of giant tortoise were penned near the offices, to be used in a captive breeding programme.

The 20-minute walk through the forest was not exactly pleasant: water came in from above, from the side and even underfoot, at times six inches deep. Birds were few and far between, with just the occasional bright red of a Madagascar fody and a few mynahs. The wet weather had encouraged the large edible snail population to come out and mating, sometimes multiple, was in full swing.

We passed wooden buildings, long abandoned, the accommodation for the Youth Programme imposed on island children in the early days of the one party socialist state. The connecting concrete roads were in good condition though the encroaching vegetation caused a deal of discomfort and it was with some relief that we arrived at the remains of the library – a two-storey structure now encased in vegetation but bone dry inside.

We took shelter among the debris and brought out the camera gear. The mosquitoes moved in immediately and insect repellent was liberally splashed on all exposed areas of skin. John had carried an aluminium set of steps as he had done a recce a few days previously and had seen a kestrel flying from the upper floor. We quietly mounted the stairs and peered around. Nothing stirred and we checked for signs. The corner which he had identified looked the most promising as there were several sets of droppings and a few pellets on the floor.

We had began to relax a bit and chat quietly when I became aware of a movement above and, sure enough, there was the kestrel up in the area between roof and wall. It shuffled out and sat in full view, wondering what was happening. I had the camera ready and took one photograph as she sat for a second before flying out and perching on a telegraph pole a few metres from the building. I quickly climbed up the steps and found three eggs in a very dry and sheltered scrape. This was probably the full clutch as equatorial falcons tend to lay much smaller clutches than their European counterparts. Other differences in the cycle include a very prolonged pre-laying period of nest inspections, supplementary feeding and copulation, and a post-fledging period of around 14 weeks when the young still receive food from the adults. This is ten weeks longer than the European kestrel takes to get the young independent. Even then, the young birds stay on territory for an average of 20 weeks after that.

*The bird slipped silently off the nest*

I had no sooner begun to descend the ladder when she came in, and flew directly onto the eggs. Setting up the camera I very gingerly retraced my steps and slowly, very slowly, inched into view. Incredibly she just sat there and looked at me so I fired off a flash shot expecting an exodus but she was totally unfazed by the whole thing. There was no holding back and I ran off the remainder of the film, using a standard lens! Fantasies are made of this.

Both John and Rosie climbed up to see her and she didn't even flinch. I eventually set up a torch to play on her to assist focussing and shot off another film just to cover myself on this one-off session. The male ventured in at one point calling but although she rose off the eggs, she stayed put and he returned to a very wet perch outside the building. The torrential rain quickly drove him to seek shelter.

*Move over! The hen was eased gently off the clutch of eggs*

I went back to the nest and she'd settled down again. It was such an experience to be able to approach this wild bird, cause no distress whatsoever and walk away leaving it at peace. Reluctantly we pulled out and ploughed our way back to the Park headquarters, oblivious of the conditions and eternally thankful for John's help. Could Mauritius better that?

A two and a half hour flight from Mahé would bring a total contrast. We were heading for only two medium-sized islands 500 miles east of Madagascar and one of the greatest population densities in the world, with 580 people per square kilometre. Our destination was the southwest corner of Mauritius, a good distance from the main tourist areas, where the rugged upland terrain still held a remnant of the tropical forest which in the 17th century clothed most of the island and supported a wealth of wildlife.

The Black River Gorge area has held a fascination for me since the early 1970s, when the Mauritius kestrel gained notoriety as the rarest bird in the world. In the past, this forest-dwelling kestrel was found throughout the island and was still common in the early 20th century despite habitat loss, unjustified persecution and the extensive use of pesticides. By 1950 the decline had begun in earnest and the bird was restricted to three mountain ranges. Ten years later it had attained the status of endangered. Loss of habitat had become acute and was

*Bambous Mountains still vegetated with trees, unlike much of Mauritius*

exacerbated by pesticide contamination as attempts were made to control agricultural pests and malaria-carrying mosquitoes. Where have we heard this before?

In addition, introduced wildlife such as mongooses and monkeys took their toll of this vulnerable and dwindling species by predating nests and killing young, which are often confiding. By 1974, the Mauritius kestrel had declined to only four known wild birds, including one breeding pair in the Black River Gorge area. They could not have been closer to oblivion and could easily have joined the dodo, which had become extinct on the island by 1651.

A conservation project was set up in 1973 and I followed its progress avidly in wildlife publications, even writing to the warden David McKelvey in 1977 to get an update of the situation. By then, the world population was down to an all-time low. David's description of their history in a letter to me highlighted the problems faced in those early dark days.

28 March 1977

Dear Mr Riddle

Thank you for your letter of 23 February. I will give you a brief run-down on the Mauritian kestrel, as you requested.

The present world population consists of 13 individuals, five of which were reared this year, Two wild pairs are productive; one at Bel-Ombre cliff in the Black River Gorges, the other in the Tamarin Gorge. In December 1976 the Bel-Ombre pair fledged three young, and the Tamarin pair fledged two.

The third remaining wild pair uses tree hole nest sites and each year is robbed by monkeys (*Macaca iris iris*).

I have a pair in captivity whose history shows a few of the problems we're up against. Captured in 1974, they laid three eggs that year. Two eggs hatched, and one young survived in an incubator until a local power surge ruined the thermostat and cooled the young bird. In 1975, one clutch of three fertile eggs was destroyed by a psychotic person. The year 1975 also gave us a three egg re-nesting, of which only one egg pipped; that one was eaten by the female.

In 1976 the breeding pair was moved to a new Government aviary site in Black River where, due to circumstances beyond my control, the breeding season was continually disturbed by construction activity. One egg was produced, but it proved infertile. The Mauritian kestrel was given a fertile American kestrel egg to hatch. She hatched it and fed it for two days, at which time she ate the baby.

The captive diet includes day-old chicks, mice, lizards and locusts. The diet in the wild is about 50% phelsuma geekos, 25% small birds (zosterops, waxbills, munias), and 25% shrews and large insects (dragonflies, mantises, beetles).

In the past, numbers of the kestrel were much higher and they ranged from coastal areas to the mountains. The decline of this fine falcon is due to the shrinking of the suitable habitat continually putting the tame, confiding kestrel into daily contact with hordes of introduced monkeys. Monkeys are regular predators on all birds' nests, and the kestrels are no exception. The surviving pairs are developing a cliff-nesting tradition which may save the species. Three years ago a pair were shot for sport by a Mauritian. (These birds allow anyone to get within 50 feet of them.)

The local government has an interest in saving the kestrels, but is unwilling to set aside and police any reserves or to destroy the monkeys. The local authority must be seen to be believed!

I hope this information will be of use to you in your work.

Sincerely yours,

*D. David McKelvey*

Just to add to the sad tale he reported that one of the wild pairs was shot by a Mauritian in 1974 and that in 1975 there had been some despondency that the remaining birds had been wiped out by Cyclone Gervaise when it hit the island, but they hung on.

It is no wonder that many people gave the Mauritius kestrel little chance of survival and that some even advocated that money would be better spent on species which were more likely to survive. The conservation programme had been sponsored by the International Council for Bird Preservation, the World Wildlife Fund and the New York Zoological Society and in 1979 a young Welshman, Carl Jones, was sent out to manage the project.

So began a critical chapter in the history of this endemic falcon. Through sheer force of character and incredible perseverance in the face of adversity, Jones not only stopped this species from falling into the abyss but gradually steered a recovery programme which has had outstanding results. Using techniques such as captive breeding, egg-pulling from breeding pairs, supplementary feeding, the fostering of young and hacking back of young to the wild, the population was slowly hauled back from the brink (Jones and Owadally 1985). The provision of artificial nest sites added to the chances of survival in areas which were particularly prone to predators and also helped the spread of the bird from the key core areas. These nest boxes were much longer than the open-fronted boxes I use. The length is critical, allowing the kestrel to nest well back out of reach of the prying arms of the macaque monkeys which had taken such a toll on the eggs and young in the years before the recovery programme started. The work progressed through the 1980s and a total of 331 kestrels were released in the ten-year period up to the 1993–1994 breeding season. One third had been captive-bred, the rest derived from eggs harvested from the wild. An astonishing and encouraging 78% of birds released survived independence.

*First encounter with a confiding Mauritius kestrel*

*Elongated nest box style to thwart the long arms of predatory monkeys*

By the 1993–1994 season, an estimated 56–68 pairs had established territories in the wild with a post-breeding population, including floating birds and independent young, of 222–281 individuals. It was decided to end the programme at that time although the population will continue to be monitored until the end of the century.

When we visited in 1997, the position was relatively stable, the population in the west standing at around 300 birds with another 100 in the east. We were about to see for ourselves the product of one of the most remarkable wildlife conservation projects of the 20th century. It was to be a culture shock and I refer to the kestrels rather than to the palms, people, beaches and beverages.

The day before we met Carl, we got a hint of the education work taking place to highlight the problems facing the endemic kestrel, pink pigeon and echo parakeet, which are still classed as vulnerable. Driving past a local school, we noticed huge murals of the three species on the walls of the building. After a lot of negotiation I managed to see the head teacher and was given permission to photograph them. No sooner had I reached the playground when the bell went and we were surrounded by eager smiling faces determined to get into the photographs. This type of outreach programme is vital in taking the local population along with the conservation projects.

*Right: No lack of children wanting their photograph taken*

*Below: Murals on school walls highlighted the indigenous species*

*Above: Spacious and well-appointed aviaries at Black River*

*Left: Endangered pink pigeon in breeding aviary*

Carl describes himself as an unusual Welshman: he doesn't like rugby and cannot sing. He is first and foremost a dedicated raptor buff with all the baggage that goes with it, and will forever be associated with the Mauritius kestrel despite all the other sterling work he and his successive teams have achieved with other endemic species on the islands. I only hope he or someone close to him will put pen to paper and write a comprehensive book on the subject. It would make fascinating reading and serve as an exemplar in conservation management.

I had seen Carl on wildlife documentaries, read his enthusiastic articles and met him at the occasional conference. Prior to the visit he had helped with the logistics of our trip and set up a meeting at the aviaries. A great deal would depend upon his response to us and it was with great anticipation that we drove down to Black River for our first meeting. Carl was late.

We were given a warm welcome by Kirsty Sunnison once we had penetrated the huge gates in the formidable walled complex which houses the Rare Birds Breeding Unit. Our first impressions of the unit, set in an attractive suburban area, were of well-constructed aviaries and roomy cage flights deliberately designed with height in mind. They housed a mind-boggling array of specialities such as Rodrigues fruit bats, echo parakeets, pink pigeons and a solitary female Mauritius kestrel suffering from rickets.

Kirsty was just pointing out a red-necked parakeet flying high towards the mountains when we heard a kestrel calling and saw it materialise in the tree in front of us. What a moment! He perched not ten metres away and nonchalantly began to preen. The plumage of the cock and hen bird are identical but, as with most falcons, the male is slightly smaller. The head and back are chestnut but it is the large, distinctive black spots on the pale breast which serve as the most outstanding characteristic. The bird was identified by Kirsty as the male of the resident breeding pair, the hen being in a nest box above us, incubating four eggs. The male was so tame that I could not resist firing off far too many photographs.

*Striking adult kestrel, curious and confiding*

Along came Carl, enthusiastic as ever, who gave us a great welcome and then promptly pulled a dead mouse out of his pocket. With Rosie reluctantly holding it, down came the kestrel and whipped the prey cleanly out of her fingers. It was a magical start. Carl explained that most of the pairs were now out in the sticks and that four pairs had moved into suburban locations, a very important step in their recolonisation of lost areas. No kestrels were now bred in captivity and the whole kestrel operation had been stood down apart from three workers, one of whom was working on the genetics side of the business.

Carl then did a tour of the compound showing us the breeding pairs of echo parakeets and the ring-necked parakeets used for staff training and for incubating echo eggs and fostering, if necessary. The attention to detail and the emphasis on cleanliness to avoid parasites was formidable. Kirsty fed one of the fruit bats by hand, which was an incredible sight, while big, colourful pink pigeons stared at us from behind wire. New units sponsored by the World Bank through the Mauritius Government were very spacious, with some flights 60 metres long. And Carl had even more plans.

All the time kestrels were coming in, perching in trees, being identified and occasionally fed. It was an amazing experience and more was to come. The birds, already tame by nature, were trained before release to respond to whistles and food, giving the fieldworker an enviable advantage in monitoring. Carl was to demonstrate this graphically.

We drove Carl into the Black River Gorge National Park, an area beset by the usual land-ownership squabbles and island politics, and pulled up on the wooded bank of a stream backed by crags. We were at one of the last remnants of the island's original vegetation cover, and a favoured habitat of the Mauritius kestrel which, unlike its counterparts in other parts of the world, is intrinsically a forest dweller. It hunts like a short-winged sparrowhawk, manoeuvring beneath the canopy to catch small birds.

We got out of the car and, within minutes of Carl calling and whistling, two kestrels appeared. As day-old chicks again appeared from his pocket, the birds flew down to collect their reward. I had a sudden image of him as a child, the archetypal nightmare boy in knee length shorts with health-hazard pockets, delving into anything and everything. This supplementary feeding had an important role to play in the recovery programme, as the extra food boosted the kestrels' diet, encouraging them to be in good condition to lay more eggs. Carl removed first clutches to hatch back in the breeding centre, confident that the wild pairs would lay a second clutch.

*Close ties were kept with released birds, with supplementary feeding a key technique.*
*The kestrel responds to Carl's whistle*

We drove up the road and once more stopped in a likely spot, passing a gamekeeper on a bike with a double-barrelled shotgun slung over his back. Poachers are not tolerated on the private hunting estates and keepers don't hesitate to shoot. Predictably enough, another two kestrels arrived to collect their free meal and leave again. It all seemed so easy until I remembered just how much work had gone into the whole scheme.

Finally we stopped opposite a crag which obviously meant a lot to Carl, who kept up a running commentary on all he saw. This was the original nesting territory where he started the recovery and the nest site was still in use. Some of the holes went back eight feet or more, and had been used for so long that when the substrate under some scrapes was analysed, the bones of prey items taken by long-extinct owls were identified. It was on this inaccessible monkey-proof cliff at Bel-Ombre in 1976 that a pair of kestrels fledged three young. At the same time, two young were fledged at the Tamarin cliff. These young kestrels became crucially important, adding vital numbers to the critically-low wild population, The other remaining wild pair had been unsuccessful for the previous five years due to monkey predation at a vulnerable site.

A single hen appeared and posed beautifully on a fence post. All these birds were known individually by Carl, a key characteristic of his work. The hen waited until the mandatory mouse had been thrown high into the air, where it was effortlessly intercepted. At that time she lacked a mate but there was by then enough of a pool of non-breeders that her chances of finding one were still good.

It had been a breathtaking introduction to the Mauritius kestrel and surpassed all expectations. Our mission was accomplished.

Late the following day, we made our way back to the Gorges but only saw kestrels at a distance and as we walked up the road could see a troop of rather large monkeys working the cliff face On cue, Carl appeared, whistled, and down came two kestrels. It would be easy to become blasé. A couple of days later, I couldn't resist whistling and - would you believe it? - in they came. What a feeling – but more was to follow.

We arrived at the aviaries on the Sunday afternoon and after reacquainting ourselves with the nesting kestrels and photographing the fruit bats which were clinging together in a sort of bee- swarm formation to keep warm, we set off to visit some of the 'whistlers" nest sites. We were accompanied by Carl and Jim, one of the team still working on the kestrel. The pick-up was abandoned near the road and we set off up a dirt track.

Jim scaled the first tree to a nest box but came back down again rather quickly as it had been colonised by bees. Carl called in the male, fed him a dead weaver bird and we moved to the next territory, passing a large baited monkey trap. The macaques are caught and legally exported. The terrain had changed and man-made rides and glades gave a much more open feel as we topped the ridge.

Halfway along the dark lava trail, we broke off and began to climb down the cliff to a lower level, passing a well-used kestrel roost site. After negotiating some quite difficult rocks, we finally came to a cave-type site with a mass of droppings coming from a dark recessed hole about 12 feet above us. The hen appeared in the nearby tree and moved closer when Carl put up a primitive ladder. As Carl began to climb, she shot into the entrance and reared up, both wings extended to protect the site before scuttling into the hole and settling on a scrape.

Rosie and I took our turn at climbing the ladder and checking her out. She was positioned well out of reach down a narrow tunnel and just sat contentedly as we admired the scene. The cavity was very deep and disappeared back into the void. It was incredible to have had a bird acting as an usherette on a visit to her nest site. Carl explained that this cave complex had been used by released slaves who, unsettled and confused by their freedom, moved initially into the hills and lived off the land.

Extricating ourselves from the caves complex, we descended the ridge and made our way round the valley, seeing plenty of monkey activity as they crossed the paths in front of us. Java

*You shall not pass!*

*At the entrance to the nest site*
*before the kestrel arrived*

deer – one of the main target species for the hunters on the private estates – were also plentiful. The going was tough, especially dressed as we were, in shorts, but we eventually descended from the cliff top and approached the last site, yet another black volcanic cliff smothered in vegetation.

Almost inevitably, the hen was above us in a tree when we made the final climb up, and again the nest hole was advertised by a mass of droppings. Carl climbed up and was immediately attacked by the hen, which gave him a good scud on top of the head, provoking some garbled Welsh expletives. I followed and was given exactly the same treatment – a well-deserved wallop. This time the nest scrape was only a few feet back and in it nestled a clutch of four.

By now the cock bird had arrived and to appease them Carl threw up a chick, only to have both birds race in, collide in mid-air, miss the prey and return to their perches. Suitably chastened, they sat in the nest tree until Carl delivered one to each of them. The hen mantled the prey then flew off to cache it. Within minutes she was back and flew straight into the nest site to cover the clutch. This was fieldwork at its most rewarding. Such is the density of the rainforest that even Carl, who has trekked this area for so many years, occasionally becomes disorientated.

The Mauritius kestrel was only one of several near-extinct species which Carl and his dedicated team were slowly but surely managing back from the brink, and we were again privileged to see their work at close quarters. We were taken to a permanent rainforest camp in a secluded area of the National Park, literally bounced there along a tortuous six kilometres of dirt track. Release pens, old and new, stood in a clearing, the former made of wood, the latter steel. This is where the birds are acclimatized and from where they are eventually released. Accommodation for the personnel was in a well-designed airy wooden building serviced by solar panels and containing a communal store, kitchen-cum-eating area and bedrooms. Basic, isolated, but perfectly fit to live in.

It was here that the famous pink pigeons started the process of being reintroduced to their natural habitat, having been captive-bred and reared in the Black River aviaries. Like the kestrel, the pigeon had reached a desperately low population level, having once been described as very common. Early Dutch settlers exploited their confiding nature to great effect to use them as a food source and by the 19th century, they were confined to forest areas. By the 1950s, they were down to a perilous 50 birds and in 1976 a captive breeding programme began in Jersey Zoo. 1993 saw a low of ten individuals in the wild.

What we were witnessing at this release point was another wonderful success story of perseverance and skill in managing a captive breeding programme under horrendous pressure. Imagine the responsibility of working with the last few individuals of a species. The work is by no means complete and the magnitude of the task ahead was brought home to us when their tameness became apparent. Photography was extremely easy as the birds were indecently approachable. The birds' natural tameness is still a major worry and the presence of trap lines for non-endemic mongooses and specially-adapted feeding tables were just two of the measures being taken to minimise casualties.

*Other indigenous species like the pink pigeon were also on the brink*

*Above: You're too close, I can't focus …*

*Left: Rosie's jewellery was a great attraction for the Echo parakeet*

No sooner had we admired the pink pigeon than a third icon came flying in to feed on the table. The cameras were again in action as an echo parakeet decided that Rosie was worth investigating and landed on her wrist, clambering confidently up onto her shoulder and trying to remove her necklace. Her face was a picture. Lance brought some fresh fruit and distracted the parakeet, as the powerful beak was beginning to make inroads into skin. Undeterred, it next began to pull apart a Kodak film box. The Danish magazine editor was taking shots as if they were going out of fashion and the bird responded by clambering all over him and his camera gear. It was hectic and Carl just stood back and enjoyed the circus, having seen it all before.

The story with the echo parakeet follows the same sad pattern as the other two. Formerly common wherever there was forest, the shrinkage of suitable habitat, allied to the negative effects of rats, introduced animals and severe storms, savagely reduced numbers. Only 15 known wild birds existed in 1991, of which only four were hens. Parasitic infections of chicks have hampered the recovery because clutches stay in the nest until they are 50 days old, but now, in yet another remarkable turnaround, there are more than 60 birds. One of the longer-term problems could be the lack of natural food as, outwith the National Park, introduced plants are gradually replacing native trees.

One interesting footnote was that the birds which we saw had bells on their legs, enabling the fieldworkers to keep in touch with them. The tame echo parakeets were a deliberate move to hold the next batch of releases in the general area of the camp, in the hope that it will become the core breeding location.

Yet more trips were made in Carl's company, one to the eastern mountains where a population of kestrels had been established from captive stock. After a long drive, we parked below an escarpment, clambered up a steep slope for a quarter of a mile until we penetrated the secondary rainforest canopy and reached the cliff line. The nest cavity was again an unusually open one and one of the boys climbed a fairly spindly tree to discover four eggs. He received the mandatory couple of clouts on the head from the hen which immediately settled once again on the eggs as soon as he had gone.

After a five minute period of grace, I was given the go-ahead and very slowly climbed the 25 feet, camera at the ready. Eventually I eased myself into position opposite her and, with great difficulty, holding on with legs only, photographed her full frame with a 200 mm lens. She just sat there, indifferent, as the flash worked away. Trying not to be greedy I slowly hauled myself down, elated once again.

As we descended, Carl lost his bearings and ending up startling a wild sow. With great dexterity, he swept up two black piglets and began to study them while Rosie and I, on the other hand, looked around for a good tree to climb should mum decide to return. Thankfully, she did not and we made it back to the truck.

The final nesting territory of the day took us to an exceptionally well-manicured hunting estate where the resident kestrel pair were using a nest box. Darrel again climbed the tree – what a luxury to have a team of climbers! – and reported a fresh scrape but no eggs as yet. Both birds suddenly appeared and sat near the box, studying us quietly. Carl decided to retrap the cock bird as the aluminum ring was getting very old, so he set up a live trap, with a small waxbill as bait, and we stood back only 30 yards away, in full sight. After a session of head bobbing, the kestrel flew down and jabbed at the trap without getting caught. He repeated this three times until at last, with a final shallow hover, he landed on the trap and was caught. The old ring was removed and measurements taken before I was given the chance to hold, then release him. Would there be no end to these experiences?

Appropriately, our final wildlife encounter of the holiday came at the Black River Gorges cave site on the last day. The aim was to photograph the hen at the site entrance and both birds were at hand when we arrived. The cock bird was soon distracted by an intruding rival, leaving the hen to deal with the domestic situation. As we set up the ladder, in she swept, making a couple of ineffective passes then diving into the nest entrance and scuttling into the darkness. Using a torch, I could see her on the first scrape. Positioning the torch so that it played on her, I

*Above: Cliff ledge site out of reach of the monkeys*

*Left: Carl with friend, two rare creatures*

*Below: It took a little while to come to terms with the size of the bird*

Adult bird caught to replace a worn ring

*I'd never imagined holding
a Mauritius kestrel ..*

*Incubating a clutch deep
inside a rock crevice*

took the first few photos. Suddenly she stood up and moved even further into the tunnel until she was standing over two eggs in a second, much safer scrape. She quickly turned them and settled down to incubate, and after a few more clicks of the camera we left. Climbing back onto the ridge, as a final gesture, I raised my arm, a chick in hand, and had it taken deftly from my fingers by the cock bird. I could not have planned a better finale.

Carl has very deservedly been awarded the MBE for his sterling work in enabling these birds to recover. The kestrel population now stands at around 1,000 birds, the figure which has been suggested as a minimum number that will maintain genetic diversity within a population and may allow, through mutation, for the restoration of any genetic impoverishment that the species may have developed while at its population bottleneck. There is little sign of severe genetic problems except for a percentage of infertile eggs.

Back home in December, with the warmth of the islands now locked away in the memory banks, a pair of kestrels began to display near my house during a spell of mild weather. Nest inspections of a nearby box were a daily occurrence before the weather closed in again and they disappeared. By my count, that made four kestrel breeding seasons in 12 months: a vintage year indeed.

# 4

## The Cape Verde Islands' kestrels

Worldwide, there are 14 species of small falcons grouped as kestrels although, as usual, that sounds more straightforward than it is. There is some disagreement as to whether the Amur falcon (*Falco amurensis*) and the red-footed falcon (*Falco vespertinis*) are genetically closer to hobbies than to kestrels. Apart from one species found in the Americas and another in Australia, they all live in Africa and Europe. Sadly, one kestrel is extinct and little is known about it: the Reunion kestrel (*Falco duboisi*) was described by Dubois in 1674 and sub-fossil bones were found on the Mascarene Islands.

Kestrels share general characteristics, such as being generalist feeders preying mostly on small birds and mammals, lizards and invertebrates. They sometimes hover when hunting, lay between two and eight eggs and do not build their own nests, and most of them, but not all, prefer open habitat types. They will tolerate close nesting and quite large aggregates if food is abundant.

They are generally long-tailed (or short-winged) and have short toes. The majority have a rufus brown plumage but there are three grey-coloured species in Africa. The fox kestrel (*Falco alopex*) is the largest of the kestrels and is three times the size of the smallest, the Seychelles kestrel. For a more comprehensive analysis of the characteristics and distribution of kestrels, I can recommend Chapter 2 of Andrew Village's book *The Kestrel*.

As you would expect, there are some very interesting traits in the kestrel family. The grey kestrel (*Falco ardosiaceus*) from Africa, for example, is largely crepuscular, being most active at dawn or dusk. One of the few birds of prey to eat vegetable matter, it will sometimes feed on oil palm nuts. The lesser kestrel (*Falco naumanni*) is the only true colonial species and one of the most stunning falcon sequences I have seen on film is of 1,200 of these birds coming in to roost in one very large pine tree in the town of Matera in southern Italy. They are abundant in the town, nesting in holes in buildings and under roof tiles.

The American kestrel (*Falco sparverius*), thought to be the most recently evolved of all the kestrels, has one of the most colourful plumages. Both sexes have two prominent black spots near the back of the head, called oculli, and many people think that they act as false eyes. The rest of the markings on the back of the head, along with the spots, possibly fool potential predators into thinking that they are seeing the kestrel's face and that the element of surprise has been lost. Head bobbing may also exaggerate this perception. The jury is still out as to whether this really is a form of disruptive or deflective coloration or whether there is another function to the design.

Captive bred American Kestrels have been extensively used in the USA and Canada for research purposes. David Bird of McGill University in Montreal has bred thousands of kestrels and these birds have contributed to studies including work on environmental toxicology, disease, embryonic growth and behaviour. Nitro, is the first falcon to be produced in captivity with frozen-thawed semen.

There are also eleven subspecies of the kestrel and, just as the bottlenecking of the Mauritius and Seychelles kestrels is fascinating, so also is the fact that the Cape Verde Islands, a small archipelago 450 miles off the West African coast, have two subspecies of the common kestrel. Remarkably, the subspecies are separated by relatively small stretches of water. This has always intrigued me and prompted me to visit the islands to see them for myself.

I decided to go in late January and early February 2010. As with any trip of this type, time spent in preparation was invaluable. I made several key contacts to help me build up a picture of what I might expect and of what would be possible.

I also began a literature check and was very lucky in several respects. Firstly, my close friends John and Doreen Melrose, who knew the authors well, gave me a copy of the David and Mary Bannerman classic *History of the Birds of the Cape Verde Islands*. This gave me a feel both for the kestrels and for the islands, as well an insight into activities which had caused declines in the past, especially on São Vicente. The almost complete disappearance of the bird from a status of abundance was attributed to the taking of young kestrels by Creole boys. The Bannermans quote Keulemans, an earlier visitor to the islands, who wrote:

> "…. the natives regard its flesh as a delicacy, especially that of the young which are usually fat …"

He did find the birds very common in the mountains.

One paragraph describes sightings on the main road to San Domingos on Santiago and I made a mental note to visit the location:

> "Our attention was directed to a regular colony of nests near the summit of the cliffs by the loud cries of the young kestrels as the parents sailed to and fro along the cliff face, when bringing the youngsters food. We could see the young in two of the nests, two in each, a third nest was close by and several other pairs were nesting on the same cliff."

They saw other pairs and concluded that it was quite a large colony, more in keeping with the lesser kestrel. It was a mouth-watering prospect.

Several scientific papers were gleaned from internet searches, including a few on the genetic structure of the kestrel populations. Roy Dennis put me in touch with one of the authors of the papers, Sabine Hille, who kindly sent me copies. (S. Hille and H. Winkler 2000 and Hille *et al.* 2003). These papers gave a clear insight into the subspecies status of Alexander's (*Falco tinnunculus Alexandri)* and neglected kestrels (*Falco tinnunculus neglectus*).

Populations of the same species often vary between the islands of an archipelago. In the case of Cape Verde, the islands in the east are very different from those in the west, the former being flat and sandy while those in the western block are less eroded and have heavily-vegetated mountains. These reach up to about 3,000 metres in addition to being the volcanic desert element. Hille and Winkler examined morphometric variation in three populations of the subspecies taking measurements from 55 living birds (Boavista 21, Santo Antao 17 and Brava 17) measuring 23 variables on the head, feet and tail.

They found significant variation in some characteristics between the subspecies, the variation occurring not just in size but also in the prey-catching features, namely the bill, talons, legs and wings. The sample of neglected kestrel (*Falco tinnunculus neglectus*) in Santo Antao had high claws, smaller bills and short, somewhat rounded wings in contrast with the bigger bill, shorter and flatter claws and more elongated wings of Alexander's kestrel (*Falco tinnunculus Alexandri*) on Boavista.

They concluded that the structural differences were an adaptation to local environments with their respective habitat characteristics, and that prey abundance played a crucial role in forming morphologically-distinct island populations. They suggested that the small bill, short rounded wing and higher talons of the *neglectus* are well adapted to capture small terrestrial prey, while the larger wing, bigger bill and flatter talons of *Alexandri* on Boavista may indicate frequent aerial hunting of larger prey items. It's quite a challenge in the field to separate these two on physical characteristics.

In the later collaborative work, Hille *et al.* looked at the genetic diversity and population structure in eight populations of the two subspecies. They analysed DNA samples from 147 kestrels between 1997 and 1999, trapping 127 live birds from seven islands compared with 20 individuals of the common kestrel from Austria.

The results indicated that *neglectus* on the northwestern islands and *Alexandri* in all the other islands were genetically-distinct units. They argued that the populations were probably founded by birds originating from the African mainland and that immigration is more likely to the eastern and southern populations than the northwestern islands where the genetic diversity was lowest.

On the whole, the Cape Verde populations exhibited lower levels of genetic diversity than those on the mainland. *Neglectus* forms a genetically distinct group while *Alexandri* could be divided into a southern and eastern group. They suggested that the differences in genetic diversity on the islands were enhanced by geographical distance between neighbouring populations and that the prevailing northeastern trade winds were not favourable for dispersing birds.

The next and probably most significant contact again came courtesy of the internet. I managed to link up with Cornelius Hazevoet, whose book *The Birds of the Cape Verde Islands* (1995) had originally sparked my interest. He was extremely helpful and put me in touch with Pedro Lopez Suarz, or 'Pedrin', who proved to be the key to the kestrels on Boavista. Pedrin and I corresponded extensively by email prior to the trip and it was a great pity that he was off the island to attend a course during our visit.

Everything came together on 25 January when, with the help of Ron Hughes and his team from Cape Verde Travel, we arrived on the island of Boavista. Boavista is one of ten islands and several islets which make up this Atlantic archipelago. Volcanic in origin, they were discovered and colonised by the Portuguese in the 15th century and are now an independent republic. The 26°C temperature was welcome after the severe winter we had just left.

We chose late winter for our trip in the hope of seeing young kestrels in the nest, as the breeding season stretches from October to the end of April. In order to maximise the time available, the strategy was first to visit Boavista, where the contacts had been made, then to

*The landscape on Boavista was mainly volcanic desert*

*First nesting cliff and the brood had flown*

spend most of the other two weeks on São Nicolau and Santo Antao in the northwest, searching for the neglected kestrel.

On the second day we made contact with Stra, a colleague of Pedrin, and on the third day of the visit set out to explore the island, hoping to get close to Alexander's kestrel in the company of Juliao, our guide for the next two days. The diary reads as follows:

> Juliao turned up promptly and we set off in the mandatory Toyota Hilux on the cobbled roads south of Sal Rei and Rabil. Our first stop was opposite a small rockface and we set off at a quick pace, despite the heat. Juliao did not speak English and our Creole was non-existent but he managed to indicate that this was a kestrel nesting territory. He had been well briefed by Pedrin and Stra and had done a lot of fieldwork with them and was familiar with several kestrel territories. Encouragingly, a kestrel circled the hill as we climbed to the nest site, a cavity in the rock which, sadly, was empty. The kestrel showed little interest in the nest site so we headed off, but only after the camera strap came loose and the camera bounced down a couple of metres. Luckily all was well.
>
> We then drove to Curral Velho in the southeast, crossing barren terrain, virtually treeless save for the odd clump of palms in the volcanic desert. The next territory had six young in the nest last month so hopes were high. We were now 'off piste' and being

*Nest site on top of the lone palm*

*Juliao checking the site*

driven along very rough tracks, putting up hoopoe larks and cream-coloured coursers. A few kilometres ahead we could see a single dead palm which had housed the brood. Once more we were thwarted as the birds had flown and all that remained was a few feathers, pellets and some broken egg shells. Juliao was very disappointed but not half as much as we were, as it had been a supposed certainty. Confidence was receding rapidly as we had seen only the one kestrel at a distance.

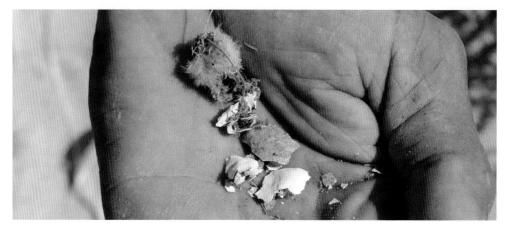

*All six birds flown, leaving only the egg shells*

Another half hour of very rough terrain took us up the coast and into a rocky basin where suddenly the complexion of the day changed dramatically. No sooner had the vehicle stopped than a pair of kestrels appeared above the cliff face, calling excitedly. First impressions were that they closely resembled the kestrel we were familiar with and I certainly could not differentiate them.

After a few impressive minutes, one of the birds, presumably the female, broke off and flew directly into a hole about three metres down from the cliff top. Juliao then went round the face and scrambled to the top. I was able to direct him to the spot before Rosie and I followed him up. Incredibly, the bird was still on the nest as we peered down. The nest was well protected in a tangle of roots and from her safe haven she just stared up at us. Luckily the cock bird called her off and we were able to see the clutch of five eggs nestling in the scrape.

In she came again, landing on a ledge and calmly scuttling back in to settle on her clutch. The cock bird flew over to a nearby face and sat preening. Photography was not easy as I had to be held as I leaned over the cliff, but she was duly recorded. I took a few more photographs of the terrain before leaving them to it, much relieved at our first result.

Using a small booklet on the birds of Cape Verde which I had borrowed from the guesthouse, Juliao pointed to the picture of the red-billed tropic bird and pointed to the coast. The text was in Portuguese but the meaning was obvious, so we set off again across the hardly-passable lunar landscape until we reached some very high sea cliffs, completing the climb on foot.

Sure enough, I picked up a couple of these stunning birds out at sea, only to see Juliao disappearing over the cliff edge. About five metres down, he signalled for us to follow. We could hear a bird calling and, against out better judgement, climbed down to the ledge, the sea crashing into the base a couple of hundred metres below. With no rope and

*Above: Both birds in attendance, a good sign*

*Right: Alexander's kestrel at close quarters*

*Below left: The hen bird settled down and watched from a distance*

*Below right: Undeterred by our presence she flew in and landed by the nest*

*The nest site was well protected by tangled vegetation*

*Juliao and Rosie down the cliff ledge*

wearing shorts, T-shirts and trainers, we were a health and safety nightmare. The tropic bird sitting on one egg was fantastic, though, and within touching distance. Photograph taken, we happily returned to the top, only for Juliao to drop down again further along. This time, Rosie declined, which was just as well as we dropped down a few metres then traversed along a pretty dodgy ledge for 20 metres more. It was worth it, though. Three nest sites, two of which could only be located by sound but a third held an adult and chick.

Glad to be back on the top again, we set out for the final cliff face. Again, a single kestrel was present in the middle of nowhere and, again, we were too late. All that remained was an addled egg. The featureless terrain did not seem capable of supporting a single bird, let alone a brood, and what vegetation there was came under severe pressure from the large number of goats. There is little data on the abundance and food habits of the kestrels but a paper by Diago Ontiveros in 2005 has shed some light on this. He found that the endemic skink accounts for 85% of the kestrel's diet on Boavista. There are four lizard species on the island but only one is diurnal. He also estimated – very roughly, as he concedes – from road transect counts that there were around 80 kestrels on Boavista.

*Tropic bird and young, deep in a crevice*

*Above: How do kestrels survive
in this bleak terrain?*

*Left: Brood flown, only an
addled egg left*

*Below: The endemic skink made
up 85% of the prey items on
Boavista*

*Large grasshoppers were part*
*of the kestrel's diet*

*An array of pellets collected below the nest*
*site in the old raven's nest*

We reached the final nesting territory after a tedious march over stony dried-up riverbeds, and it ended with a blank. Still, we had no complaints: the day had been superb. Could the next day be as productive?

28 January 2010

The weather was still superb and off we went, this time covering the southwest of the island. Just south of Sal Rei, we pulled off into some mixed scrub and palm habitat and homed in on a palm which had a very inviting nesting cavity halfway up the trunk. It was empty but was an excellent example of the type of site used by the kestrels. What a luxury to have someone else climbing trees!

After a long and rough journey, we were into different landscape: gravel, sand and dunes with quite a lot of ground cover and a smattering of palms. Off-road again and we picked up a kestrel perched on a palm tree. As the vehicle approached, three juveniles took to the air and began flying around, calling. The nest was in an old brown-necked raven's stick platform near the top of a palm. Pellets and droppings covered the ground below.

Using the vehicle as cover, we slowly crept up on two of the birds which had settled on another tree a few hundred metres away. The cautious approach paid off and we took several photographs before the adults called them into the air again.

Moving to the coast, we found another nest, this time in an inaccessible hole in the cliff face. I was very satisfied as I found the nest while the others were exploring one of the several sea caves. The sandy track took us back up the coast and a pair of ospreys sitting on a nest on an off-shore rocky plinth, plus five green turtles feeding in the bay. It was almost our 'Thelma and Louise' moment as Juliao stopped the vehicle perilously close to the cliff edge!

Parking on the sandy cliff top, we made our way very slowly round a small hill, finding ourselves right on top of a hen kestrel which just sat on the cliff top as we closed in. She only took off calling when we were within five metres and we were able to look over the cliff and see two nearly full-grown chicks in a very messy nest ledge. While we stayed on

96

Clockwise from left: Juliao was adept at tackling the climbing chores

The brown-necked raven was common and its old nests were regularly used by the Alexander's kestrel

The hen bird was perfectly relaxed at our approach

Finally she reacted but still did not back off

Two newly-fledged young were quite confiding

*Above: Kestrel nest below. Note the previous year's osprey nest on the left*

*Left: Two large young and an addled egg nestled on the ledge below*

the cliff top, Juliao went further along the coast to get a photograph for himself and ended up on a rocky outcrop opposite the ledge. To get his shot, he stood on an old osprey nest! No sooner had we moved back off the cliff line than she returned to her original perch and proceeded to scold us. Amazing.

Juliao had done a great job, considering the language difficulties and the fact that the kestrel does not feature as one of the fieldwork priorities of the Naturalia conservation group which he works for. Pairs of kestrels were found by chance when they survey the island's ospreys. From what I could glean from Pedrin, the main threats to the kestrel are the brown-necked raven, feral cats and human disturbance. The productivity seems good, with clutches of four to six being normal.

As a footnote to *Alexandri*, we did stop over for a couple of days on Santiago and travelled along the San Domingos road. The cliffs were impressive but, alas, the colony of kestrels described by the Bannermans was gone and we did not see a single bird. At least, though, my mental picture of the colony is now real. The compensation was the mandatory pilgrimage to the colony of Bourne's purple heron (*Ardea purpurea bournei*), the fledged young hanging about the canopy of two mahogany trees. We also had the bonus of numerous sighting of the grey-headed kingfisher, the Cape Verde Islands' national bird. This superbly-coloured bird is not aquatic and is found in well-vegetated valleys and cultivated areas where it feeds not on fish, but on invertebrates and small lizards.

*San Domingos cliffs, mentioned by the Bannermans as a possible colony of Alexander's kestrels*

*Left: The national bird, a grey-headed kingfisher, was common*

*Below: Very different terrain on São Nicolau: heavily vegetated mountain slopes*

We moved on to São Nicolau, one of the north islands inhabited by the neglected kestrel. This was a much tougher proposition. The terrain was totally different and cold searches were the order of the day, as I had not managed to set up any contacts or glean any definitive information on the kestrel population. It proved to be a huge challenge.

Although kestrels were seen regularly as we moved round the island, they were distant views, giving very little clue as to their lifestyle, and the chance to get close to the birds looked slim. The steep, wooded mountainsides were virtually impossible to penetrate. After the first few days, the only impression I had was that the bird did confirm to the taxonomic descriptions and had rounder wings than *Alexandri*, and that it was reasonably common, if well spaced out.

A visit to the Monte Gordo National Park illustrated the problem. We located three pairs but access to the cliff faces was prohibitive. The birds did hunt on the lower ground among the small cultivated plots which had been integrated into the park when it was designated – these smallholdings were inundated with invertebrates and the kestrels seemed to perch-hunt more frequently than hover, although it had been recorded – but a single photograph of birds at a distance demonstrated the problem we faced.

*The small holding pattern in Monte Gordo National Park provided ideal foraging areas for the neglected kestrel*

*After five days this was the nearest we had come to kestrels*

On the second to last day, we decided that the best strategy was to spend the bulk of our time simply roaming the periphery of the park near its headquarters, observing kestrel activity in an area where more sightings had been made. It paid off. At first it felt as if we were wasting our time as although by using the vantage points we located two pairs, we had to watch food passes, flying in and out of possible nest sites, mobbing ravens and even display from a distance. The break came as we moved position and a bird was seen perch-hunting from a tree at the edge of a bean crop. I managed to approach the bird through the low vegetation and at last got a photograph. The bird then moved about the area, using rock outcrops and palm trees as perches before dropping to the ground and catching insects. It was feeding very regularly and catching on just about every drop. Then a second kestrel, presumably its mate, flew in calling and off they went.

At last, a co-operative Falco neglectus

Perch hunting from a palm tree at the edge of the fields

Back at the roadside, we were chatting to park staff when I spotted another bird on one of the telephone poles. Walking slowly towards it, I soon realised that it was totally focussed on the adjacent field. It let me get very close before dropping into the beans, picking up a large grasshopper and flying off. Yet another bird appeared on the wires outside the park headquarters, proceeding to juggle to stay balanced and concentrate on the ground below. The drop was successful and it ate the large black beetle on the spot.

*Above: This bird used the line of roadside poles to great effect*

*Above right: Intense concentration before the drop*

*Right: Beetle safely in the talons*

In the next hour, we observed several more hunting attempts, the only casualty being my socks which were so covered in burrs and other seeds from wandering among the undergrowth that I left them behind in a litter bin. The day's efforts, though, had been well worthwhile.

Apart from the taxonomic and genetic work described earlier, there is very little information on the neglected kestrel. We spent a further five days on Santo Antao and the pattern was the same: plenty of sightings, but only at a distance. The only piece of data of any relevance was that all the birds seen, bar none, were perch-hunting. Again, the favoured hunting habitats were the well-vegetated valleys, with extensive use of low-lying crops on hillside terraces and irrigated fields. Like *Alexandri,* the pairs seemed well spaced out due to the mountainous nature of the ground. They were seen from sea level up to 1500 metres where one pair was seen displaying and mobbing ravens.

*Above: Mountainous
terrain on Santo Antao*

*Right: Perch hunting was almost
exclusively used by the neglected
kestrels we observed*

*Below: Terraced plots favoured
by the kestrels as hunting spots*

In summary, both subspecies seem widespread at present over their particular islands, pairs being readily visible, and it was fascinating to observe the kestrel in a totally different environment. The differences in the subspecies were subtle and without genetic analysis and the ability to take measurements of a bird in the hand, differentiation apart from wing shape was difficult. There is, though, a lack of hard information on distribution, population sizes and trends and breeding data, and this is worth flagging up as the islands are changing. In the light of the rapid expansion of the tourist industry, which could in the future have an impact on the kestrels, a database and ongoing monitoring would be extremely valuable. This is particularly appropriate for the Alexander's kestrel as its nest locations are much more vulnerable compared with those of the high-living *neglectus*. From personal experience, I can fully understand why it is called the neglected kestrel.

*Profile of neglected kestrel in flight, showing the rounded wings*

# 5

## *The newsworthy kestrel*

The common kestrel has one of the highest profiles of any of Britain's raptors, its characteristic mode of hunting, quirky nest site choices and general empathy with urban life guaranteeing it a place in the public eye and frequent media appearances.

Its hovering profile also lends itself to interesting logo designs and many organisations have adopted the kestrel as a brand, the most famous being the lager link. Bill Oddie models the Kestrel waistcoat. You can grow Kestrel potatoes, follow the Australian netball team, the Melbourne Kestrels, and even go to the Kestrel Hydro, a naturist spa near Heathrow Airport. The Kestrels, a British band first formed 50 years ago, were one of the busiest vocal groups of the late 1950s and early 1960s, singing back-up to legends such as Joe Brown, Billy Fury, Benny Hill and even the Beatles.

I have collected some of the most interesting snippets which give a slightly different insight into the bird's lifestyle and its relationship with man.

### *The twitcher's tale, part 1*

November 1994 and birdline pagers were red hot. For only the third time in the century, a Blyth's pipit had arrived in Britain from Siberia and was hanging out at Landguard Point near Felixstowe. The bird is notoriously difficult to identify as it is virtually impossible to distinguish it from the closely-related Richard's or the tawny pipit. This major hurdle had been overcome as the bird in question had been trapped by the local warden, authenticated and released to face an impressive battery of tripods, cameras, binoculars and telescopes. What happened next was succinctly described by Brian Morton in *Scotland on Sunday* as a 'miniature ornithological snuff movie'. Enter one hungry kestrel and exit, in full view of admiring eyes and with a hundred more avid twitchers still on their way to see it, one very, very rare Blyth's pipit. Emotions ran high and for once the kestrel's popularity among this fraternity sank to rock bottom. Still, on the positive side, it was a new record on the kestrel's prey list for Britain.

*The twitcher's tale, part 2*

## Bill Oddie's Little Black Book

In September 1979 while I was filming a TV show near Portland Bill Bird Observatory – a location chosen quite coincidentally by the BBC, with absolutely no pressure from me – I was lucky enough to find a yellow-billed cuckoo, a rare visitor from America. The bird was rather elusive but by the evening, about four or five birders from the observatory had also managed to see it. Announcement of its arrival was not actually broadcast on *Nationwide* – indeed no effort was made to spread the news, as the bird was on private farmland. Nevertheless, by dawn the next morning there were two hundred twitchers lined up along the side of the field waiting for the bird to reappear – which, being a Yankee exhibitionist, it did. That's how efficient the grapevine is. And such is the attraction of a rare bird that by the end of the cuckoo's four or five day stay, it was estimated that at least a thousand twitchers had ticked it off. And yet perhaps even more mysterious is the way the negative grapevine works equally efficiently. On the Friday afternoon, the cuckoo was seen being eyed by a hungry-looking kestrel. At one point the kestrel actually grabbed it and carried it off, only to be pursued by a gang of anxious twitchers, who so moved the falcon with their howls of dismay that it dropped the rarity immediately. Not surprisingly, however, the cuckoo decided to quit Dorset that evening. Saturday's sun dawned on two or three hundred twitchers, who, by ten o'clock, were close to tears as they had to accept that their quarry had either flown or had literally been scared to death by the kestrel.

*Free food and pipedreams*

The little tern colony at Great Yarmouth, which holds 10% of the British population of 2,400 pairs, has suffered badly from the usual predation – hedgehogs which eat the eggs and kestrels which take the chicks. Three pairs of kestrels, which nested within range of the colony in 1992, accounted for 143 chicks and clearly some initiative was needed to reduce this level of predation, or the consequences would be severe.

When two pairs of kestrels began to plunder the colony the following year, the decision was taken to supply the kestrels with an alternative food source – laboratory-bred mice – which were dropped directly into the kestrel nests. Preliminary results from this diversionary feeding would seem to indicate success as when the supply was constant, the birds did not travel to the colony and when, as a control measure, the artificial food source was stopped, they reverted to hunting the colony. The end result was that, in 1992, 176 young little terns were fledged, a great improvement on the previous two years when 12 and 15 were the worrying totals.

As a conservation measure it seemed to work well. The results of later feeding experiments, switching food on and off within a season and providing food in alternate years, do suggest that supplementing feeding is likely to be an effective tool for increasing the productivity of little tern colonies threatened by kestrel predation. The downside is that the technique is time consuming, expensive and has the potential to create a queue of kestrels vying to hold these prime territories!

In 1996 the total failure of the colony due to a combination of high tides and predation resulted in a review of the best available protection methods. The following year the wardens employed a clever technique to thwart the kestrels and deal with strong sand blows which together had caused problems in the past.

*Pipe to give little terns protection from hunting kestrels*

Wooden shelters, two sections of plywood joined at 90º, had been used to shelter the chicks but the design had been flawed. Even while the chicks were in the havens, the kestrels merely landed on the beach and, stretching in with their claws, extracted their prey from the shelters. Having seen plastic pipes being used successfully for common tern chicks at a Yorkshire Wildlife Trust reserve at Denaby Ings, Mark Thomas and Jeremy Atkins decided to give this a try at North Denes.

They camouflaged the pipes by covering them in glue then rolling them in sand, and also sprayed them with colours which blended in with the colony environs. Two hundred shelters were placed in the colony on 25 May, in a random arrangement, although they were placed about 15 feet away from known nests. The lower part of the pipe was sunk into the sand to a level which prevented predation by ground-attacking kestrels.

Three days after the colony's first hatch, several chicks began using the shelters and the habit was soon widespread. Multiple use by different families became commonplace. As in previous years, supplementary feeding of kestrels helped to reduce the level of little tern predation but it was clear that the provision of the shelters had led to a significant cut in chick loss. Only once was a kestrel seen taking a chick from the entrance of a shelter. In 1997, 191 pairs fledged 135 chicks.

*Carnage on the rigs: the real Buchan budgies*

The habit of kestrels using oil platforms as feeding stations is alluded to in my previous book, and a report from the North Sea Bird Club quarterly bulletin covering the autumn of 1992 illustrates just how prevalent this is.

### *The Fulmar*, North Sea Bird Club Quarterly Bulletin No. 70

When Peter Dale returned to the Buchan Alpha platform on 24 September, two juvenile kestrels were in residence, feeding on the plentiful supply of small birds. By late afternoon on the 25th, prey had become scarce and one bird moved on. The remaining bird began to feed from the surface of the sea and was seen on one occasion taking a goldcrest which had just fallen in. The bird did not feed off carrion on the platforms, despite its availability, but did take bodies from the surface of the water. Later that afternoon, a bonxie arrived and began to harass the kestrel but to no avail as the falcon fed on the wing, even while the dogfight was in progress.

*Kestrel caught on Hewett platform*

Over the next few days the number of kestrels built up to three males and three females, joined on the 30th by two merlins. One sparrowhawk arrived in poor condition and was caught and transported to the beach. Another arrived the next day and was hounded off by two of the kestrels. By the next day, only two male kestrels remained but they were joined by two females on the 5th, 'slaughtering everything in sight, flying through and even perching on the crane booms when they were in motion … dodging round the drier package and hovering only feet about the main deck … leaving most of the crew spellbound. The need to wear a hard hat became obvious when one guy almost had his hair parted!'

The platform emblem, referred to as the 'Buchan Budgie', is in the form of a 'Prussian eagle in drag', the design of which was stimulated by visits from kestrels to the platform when it was in Stornoway being converted to its present form. Despite trying, I have unfortunately been unable to get a photograph of the intriguing image!

## Pee at your peril

### *New Scientist*, 4 February 1995

Experiments with captive kestrels at the University of Turku in Finland indicate strongly that voles' urine plays a significant role in their predation. The theory is that these small rodents, which mark their environment with urine trails to aid navigation and communication, are detected because the marks are visible in ultraviolet light. Birds have five or six different kinds of cones in their retinas and can perceive ultraviolet light, allowing them to home in on these giveaway signs. The researchers, led by Erkki Korpimäki, allowed kestrels to hunt over areas which were either clean or impregnated with vole urine trails. These areas were lit with UV light and the kestrels showed most interest in the latter. They also laid trails in areas where vole numbers were scarce, attracting kestrels which hunted in vain for prey. The Finns believe that kestrels use UV vision to focus their hunting on areas that contain large numbers of voles. If this is the case, then it's little wonder that the vole is the preferred prey item of the kestrel and other avian predators.

*The short-tailed field vole is undoubtedly the kestrel's main prey*

## Kestrel in a Basket

### *The Sunday Post*, 11 July 1999

One of the club members at the Rosemount Golf Course near Blairgowrie was looking in the rough for his wayward ball when he found a young kestrel. It looked quite healthy so he left it where it was and the parents were seen feeding it on the ground. The bird had obviously prematurely vacated the nest high in the tree off the first fairway. But later that night, the bird-loving golfer decided that it would not be safe to leave the bird on the ground at the mercy of predators so he fashioned a substitute nest out of an old hanging basket he found in the garage.

He nailed it to the tree, lined it with straw and put the fledgling inside. The adults were completed unconcerned and readily fed the bird in its makeshift platform. Two weeks later, fully feathered, it took to the air. Birdies are common on most golf courses, eagles less so and albatrosses much rarer but this must go down as a kestrel in one.

## *A kestrel at 60 m.p.h.*

### *The Sun*, 18 May 1999

A motorist was spotted hurtling along at 60 m.p.h. while birdwatching through binoculars. The driver was nabbed by traffic police during the first week of Scotland's Speedwatch campaign. They saw him weaving all over the country road in the Borders as he leaned out of the window, steering with one hand while watching a kestrel through the field glasses. A police spokesman said, "His eyes were on the bird and nothing else. It was unbelievably stupid." The man was charged with careless driving.

## *Leicester City box*

### *Green* magazine, January 1992

Leicester City Football Club has gone green. Groundstaff there have taken up the environmental challenge by starting to use organic fertilizer on the pitch and they've even erected a kestrel nesting box on one of the ground's floodlight pylons. The new era has been ushered in by an environmental policy statement drawn up by the club as part of Leicester's Environmental City campaign.

## *World's rarest falcon gobbles up world's rarest pigeon*

### *British Birds* vol 88. no 2. p122

A predicament indeed! News came through last autumn from Save Animals from Extinction, the official appeal of the Jersey Wildlife Preservation Trust, that on the islet of Ile aux Aigrettes off the coast of Mauritius, fieldworkers were celebrating as a new generation of the pink pigeon (*Columba mayeri*) considered the world's rarest pigeon, was beginning to hatch. Suddenly one of the world's rarest falcons, the Mauritius kestrel (*Falco punctatus*) swooped down on the nest and devoured one of the squabs. Carl Jones, the Project Director, is said to have raised a rum to the balance of nature being restored, but it was promptly interfered with again when the culprit kestrel was caught and banished to a forest site on mainland Mauritius.

*Ironic that one rarity was the victim of another equally-scarce bird*

*Roadside Refuge*

*New Scientist*, **4 March 2000**

Predatory birds prefer roadsides to open fields, and the busier the road the better, say French biologists. In fact, the birds would rather hunt near thundering autoroutes than quiet country lanes because the constant traffic disturbs them less.

Birdwatchers have known for years that predators like to hunt on roadside verges. But until now, nobody realized that they have a preference for certain types of road. In fact, it had always been assumed that quieter roads were more likely to be chosen as hunting grounds because there is less risk of being hit by a car.

To find out more, Francis Meunier and his colleagues at the Chizé Centre for Biological Studies looked at the distribution of kestrels, buzzards and black kites on an intensively-farmed plain 100 kilometres north of Bordeaux. They found that all three birds preferred roads to farmland, and that all preferred the four-lane A10 autoroute to a quiet country lane.

Meunier believes this has something to do with adaptation to traffic disturbance. 'The volume of traffic on motorways does not seem to be a concern, probably because it is a routine disturbance,' he says. 'The birds have the habit of seeing fast traffic all the time and they integrate it. But on quiet roads, slower vehicles are not habitual. Kestrels seemed more disturbed by our car driving slowly – they sometimes flew away when we passed.'

The A10 has other attractions, the team says. Shrubs that were planted when it was built are reaching optimal perching height, and the verges have plenty of open areas for hunting. And for the scavenging black kite, more cars mean more roadkill.

Meunier says the findings suggest that motorway verges could be managed to help conserve birds of prey, especially in areas of intensive agriculture. Buzzards are quite common, but kestrels are in decline and black kites are on the European Union's priority list of endangered species.

'Motorways are already helping,' says Meunier. But he warns that the verges will need to be managed properly. In particular, he says, there is a danger of the shrubs growing so tall and dense that they turn into a forest. 'That's not good for raptors – they need a mixed habitat.'

Britain's Royal Society for the Protection of Birds has greeted the study with caution. 'My worry is that people will use this to demonstrate how good roads and cars are for the environment,' says Julian Hughes of the Species Policy Unit. 'It's good that there's still somewhere for these birds to feed. But the fact that it's a motorway verge is a damming indictment of the rest of the countryside.'

*Common kestrel takes canary from cage*

*British Birds* **95, January 2002**

On 12 December 1998, in Los Cristianos, Tenerife, Canary Islands, I saw an adult male common kestrel (*Falco tinnunculus)* take a canary (*Serinus canaria*) from a cage suspended on the outside wall of an apartment block. The kestrel held the canary in its right talon, while plucking the finch through the bars of the cage. I watched this activity for about five minutes, and eventually the kestrel let the canary, by then dead, fall to the bottom of the cage. After hanging upside-down on the bars of the cage, the kestrel swooped up to perch on a similar nearby cage, which contained another, terrified canary. The latter was saved by the appearance of the occupant of the first-floor flat, causing the kestrel to fly off.

*Kestrel rescue adds sponsor to helpline*

### Cage and Aviary Birds, 6 October 2001

A young female kestrel found by workers on a demolition site in Stratford, east London, has brought Raptor Rescue some good fortune in the shape of a new sponsor for its national helpline.

The bird, nicknamed Erica, was brought to Raptor Rescue's bird of prey hospital in Hertford by Community Relations Officer Louise Donkin. Louise is employed by civil engineering company Skanska UK, which is currently involved in the construction of several sections of the Channel Tunnel Rail Link, a high-speed link from St Pancras to the Kent coast.

It was on part of the huge Stratford construction site that a pair of kestrels had raised their brood of two youngsters, which were about to fledge. One of the fledglings was able to fly to safety, but Erica wasn't ready to take to the air and ended up on the ground. She was rescued by one of the workers and put in a safe place, whilst Skanska's environmental team tried to find her a suitable refuge.

It was Louise's colleague Andy Fletcher who saved the day. Andy is keen on birds of prey and had previously been on falconry experience days at the Hawk Conservancy. Andy put in a call to Ashley Smith's bird of prey centre in Hampshire and they quickly passed on the Raptor Rescue national helpline number, which Andy immediately rang.

It wasn't long before the kestrel was in the care of Raptor Rescue's vice-chairman George Duncalf. Louise drove to Hertford herself to deliver Erica and was so impressed by the work of the charity that she promised to try to help with some of the funding. True to her word, when Louise and Andy returned several days later to take part in releasing Erica back to the wild, she was pleased to announce that Skanska had agreed to sponsor the Raptor Rescue national helpline for one year.

*A sparrowhawk's tail*

### Cage and Aviary Birds, 13 January 2005

A kestrel is learning to fly again after having new feathers implanted in its tail. Kes was found starving and exhausted by a farmer at Weeley Heath, near Colchester, Essex. His tail feathers were missing after being burnt off by the toxic effect of pig slurry, leaving the bird grounded and unable to catch food.

He was taken to the Wild Lives rescue centre at Thorrington, Essex, where he was fed through a tube and brought back to full strength, but his missing feathers meant that he was still unable to fly.

Rescue centre owner Rosie Catford was anxious to get the bird back into the wild as soon as possible so she contacted the Suffolk Owl Sanctuary, which stepped in to offer a solution.

'They said they had feathers which they had saved from birds of prey they had dealt with. They suggested these could be used to replace the feathers Kes had lost,' said Miss Catford.

However, as no kestrel feathers were available, they had to use sparrowhawk feathers. The operation to superglue them into the bird's tail took three hours and was the first time the Centre had attempted the procedure.

Miss Catford said it had been a complete success and that within 24 hours, Kes had been flying around his pen.

*Kestrels halt work on £52 million project*

**Cage and Aviary Birds, 8 July 2004**

Four nestling kestrels have almost completely halted work on Cheshire's Thelwall viaduct after the adult pair took up residence. As a protected species they must, by law, be left undisturbed, so engineers have had to reschedule work on the structure, continuing work elsewhere until the kestrels finish nesting. The engineers are replacing worn out bearings on the busy bridge which carries tens of thousands of vehicles a day across the River Mersey and Manchester Ship Canal at Warrington. The £52 million project is not expected to be finished for another year. The engineers said they were delighted to help the birds.

*Using barn owls and kestrels for agricultural biological pest control on both sides of the Jordan River*

**Falcon, the newsletter of the Middle East Falcon Research Group, issue 34, Autumn 2009**

Barn owls and kestrels in Israel are being used as agricultural pest controls in order to reduce the use of pesticides and their negative impacts. In 1983 the first nest boxes for barn owls were erected and in 2000 the project was expanded to include kestrels, with approximately 100 nest boxes erected throughout Israel.

Work by Mattie Charter in his MSc at Tel Aviv University discovered that 76% of the kestrel prey in the Bet-Shi'an Valley consisted of voles and other rodents. The constant 24-hour threat of predation by the diurnal kestrels and nocturnal barn owls caused changes in the prey's behaviour, resulting in their spending less time foraging and damaging crops.

In 2002 a joint professional seminar was held in Israel for Israeli and Jordanian scientists and farmers to put over the concept. In the Muslim tradition, barn owls symbolize bad luck and many of the Jordanian farmers were at first hesitant to co-operate. Yet after a few farmers used barn owls instead of chemical pesticides with tremendous success, others were quick to follow suit. During 2005–2008, the project was expanded beyond the borders of the country and 37 nest boxes were erected in Jordanian fields to the east of the Jordan River.

In parallel, ten barn owl nest boxes were erected in the fields of Jericho in the Palestinian Authority and a three-year research project was funded to compare the results in experimental wheat fields with and without pest control by barn owls and kestrels in Israel, Jordan and the Palestinian Authority. In June 2007, the General Directors of the Ministry of Agriculture and Ministry of Environmental Protection decided to promote a three-year national project (2008–2010) using barn owls and kestrels countrywide in Israel.

It is hoped that this idea will be developed as a national project which will be joined by hundreds of farmers in Israel and as a regional project with the Palestinians and Jordanians. The aim is to significantly expand the scope of the use of nest boxes in Jordan and the Palestinian Authority during 2009–2011. Even more ambitious is the possible extension of the project further afield to African countries thus developing a cross-continental environmental concept that will decrease the harm to local and migrating birds.

*Barn owl ambush*

**Birdwatching 6 March 2009**

The barn owl and kestrel normally coexist but wildlife photographer Damian Waters caught

*Don't mess with my airspace ...*

on camera a pair of kestrels mugging a barn owl. His superb set of photographs show a pair of kestrels harassing a barn owl which was making a daytime sortie during a winter cold snap when food was in short supply. Mr Waters said, 'It was incredible to watch. A pair of kestrels had obviously learnt the barn owl's routine and I observed them sitting on opposite sides of a field watching the hunt. As soon as the barn owl swooped on prey, the kestrels would come screaming in and bully the owl off the prey item. This happened several times until the kestrels had eaten enough and the owl finally got to eat its catch. I have seen the owl since and it looks in rude health so it survived the dogfight and has obviously been able to feed itself in the Arctic conditions.'

*Both kestrels were heavily engaged in the attack*

In this series of encounters, the enterprising kestrel's aggression really paid dividends. This type of piracy has been reported on several occasions in various ornithological journals with a variety of combinations – kestrel robbing barn owl, kestrel robbing merlin, red-footed falcon robbing kestrel.

## Kestrels fast food – snipe and swift

Two examples of the catholic feeding habits of kestrels. Simon Barns in a letter to *BBC Wildlife* magazine in May 2000 recounts:

'It happened at Blacktoft Sands RSPB reserve in northeast Lincolnshire. A male kestrel came towards our hide, flying about two metres above the ground, and two of a group of snipe took to the air. The kestrel dived on the remaining snipe at the water's edge and pinned it to the ground. The snipe eventually died after about five minutes and the kestrel had a good feed. It then grasped the dead snipe in its talons and made short flights of about a yard at a time, finally stashing it in some tufts of grass. The kestrel came back later just before dusk and had another feed. It was an opportunist kill rather than intended. But it was a rare event, and you certainly do not read of kestrels taking snipe in any of the bird books.'

The second incident, reported in issue 9 of *De Takkeling* was more athletic and impressive. On 10 June 2001 a hovering male kestrel suddenly dropped and captured one of many passing swifts which were feeding at low altitudes above a wetland in the northern Netherlands. Plucking took some 20 minutes before the bird returned to the nest box with its prey. This capture was considered a lucky try.

## Another Opportunist

### Bird Watching, April 2002

Unusual feeding behaviour was reported by Joanna Fort of Barnoldswick who asked. "Have any other readers got such a cheeky mealworm stealer? I'm used to wrens, robins and dunnocks but now we have this kestrel regularly. We also have two brave jays which feed on the wall behind the kestrel!"

## Kestrel at Number 10

### You Tube, News and Politics

On 9 July 2008, a young kestrel was rescued in the garden of 10 Downing Street. Nicknamed PJ, it had been abandoned by its mother and was at risk from crows, cats and torrential rain. The Royal Parks' wildlife expert cared for it but, despite a promise to keep interested parties up to date, I have been unable to find out if the bird survived and was released back into the wild.

## Windhover

### Gerard Manley Hopkins, 1844–1889

> I caught this morning morning's minion, kingdom of daylight's dauphin, dapple-
> dawn-drawn Falcon, in his riding
> Of the rolling level underneath him steady sir, and striding

High there, how he rung upon the rein of a wimpling wing
In his ecstasy! Then off, off forth on swing,
As a skate's heel sweeps smooth on a bow-bend: the hurl and gliding
Rebuffed the big wind. My heart in hiding
Stirred for a bird, - the achieve of, the mastery of the thing!
Brute beauty and valour and act, oh, air, pride, plume, here
Buckle! AND the fire that breaks from thee then, a billion
Times told lovelier, more dangerous, O my chevalier!

No wonder of it: sheer plod makes plough down sillion
Shine, and blue-bleak embers, ah my dear,
Fall, gall themselves, and gash gold-vermilion.

## RSPB to Hawk and Owl Trust – transfer

### Peregrine, Autumn 2009

I must admit it was with great sadness that I learnt that the RSPB had dropped the YOC's familiar logo of a hovering kestrel in favour of one featuring red admiral, otter, barn owl and great crested grebe. The aim is 'to improve recognition of the world's largest youth organisation'. Thankfully, the Hawk and Owl Trust has filled the kestrel gap by developing its Kestrel Club for younger members.

The Trust has also launched a Kestrel Highways Project, aiming to put up 240 nest boxes along 240 miles of road. The project hopes to see whether lack of nesting sites is at the heart of the kestrel's decline in the UK. After installing the first ten nest boxes last year on the A38 north of Bristol, the South Gloucestershire group produced a leaflet and A4 poster which they have distributed within communities along the A38. The same grant also paid for a display board for use at events. There was no take-up of the group's boxes in 2009 but 60% of the new Highways nest boxes on the A303 in Wiltshire were occupied by breeding pairs.

## Kestrels on the highways

### Birder's World, April 1999

In 1983, Ron Andrews, a wildlife biologist with the Iowa Department of Natural Resources, and Trent Bales, a teenager working on his Eagle Scout badge, originated Iowa's interstate highway nest box programme for American kestrels. They erected nest boxes on the back of information signs along the I-35 in northern Iowa. These nest boxes now dot every mile of the I-35 in Iowa, representing the first state-wide kestrel trail along the interstate system.

The idea caught on and other biologists in Minnesota and Nebraska also introduced highway nest box projects in the mid-1980s. Today, kestrel nest boxes are monitored along the interstates and highways in more than a dozen US states and Canadian provinces. The figures are impressive. In Georgia, John Parrot, Professor of Biology at Georgia Southern University, monitors 200 nest boxes along the I–16. In Iowa, eight of the 20 original boxes were used by kestrels during the first year and, in the 15 years since the programme started, the kestrels using the 290 boxes have produced more than 6,500 young kestrels. An incredible statistic.

*Who is the lodger?*

The pictures tell it all. Young kestrels and barn owls happily coexisting in the same nest box. This happened in Boston, Lincolnshire in 2009 and could be the result of a lack of nest sites in the area. The feeding and calling must have been incredible. How did both sets of young respond to different parents in what must have been a 24-hour feeding regime? Oh, to have had a camera inside that nest box! The fact that both species feed on similar small mammal prey items must have been a positive factor. Seemingly, both species used the box the previous year. The kestrel pair fledged four young: I do not know the outcome for the barn owl and brood, but the adult kestrels were seemingly harassing the adult owls as they tried to return to the box.

*The nest box with barn owl and kestrel chicks just visible*

*Incredible example of shared accommodation*

The up-to-date news is fascinating. In 2010, the kestrels laid a clutch of five eggs in the nest box but, alas, the owls do not appear to have taken up permanent residence. The female has been in the box several times. The kestrel has laid the clutch just inside the entrance to the box and although the owls have been seen in the trees nearby, they do not seem to be able to get in past the kestrel.

There are plenty of records of these species nesting very close together in buildings, trees, barns and haystacks and there is even another instance of their breeding together in dual nest boxes erected as a result of the Barnsley Biodiversity Habitat Action Plan. As part of the kestrel and barn owl Species Action Plans, 12 nest boxes were put up in 2006 and 2007, and in 2007 half the boxes were used by visiting barn owls. During the breeding season, four boxes were occupied by barn owls and four by kestrels. In one box, however, a barn owl pair nested in the lower part and the kestrels in the apex roof section.

## Common kestrel attempting to predate hobby chicks at the nest

**British Birds, April 2010**

In July 2009, my wife and I watched a common kestrel (*Falco tinnunculus*) twice attempt to take young from the nest of a hobby (*F. subbuteo*) in Willingham by Stow, Lincolnshire. The nest was an old carrion crow's (*Corvus corone*) nest, about 10 metres from the ground in an ash tree (*Fraxinus excelsior*) in the middle of open farmland. I had watched the nest daily since 14 June and in that time seen both hobbies, but usually the female, aggressively mob any potential predator that came too close to the nest, including grey heron (*Ardea cineren),* common buzzard (*Buteo buteo)*, lesser black-headed gull (*Larus fuscus)* and carrion crow.

At 1935 hours on 30 July, a female kestrel landed in a barley field about 15 metres from the nest and was immediately mobbed by the female hobby. Instead of being forced away from the area, however, the kestrel flew towards and landed at the top of the nest tree, about three metres above the nest. The hobby dived repeatedly at the kestrel, calling constantly, but the kestrel seemed unperturbed. When the kestrel took off, it hovered very briefly, then suddenly flew fast and direct, straight at the nest. The hobby chased it and managed to come between the kestrel and the nest at the last moment; the kestrel was close enough to stretch out a talon toward the three chicks, which were by that time 16–18 days old, before aborting the attempt.

Some five minutes later, the kestrel reappeared and again landed at the top of the tree just above the nest; the adult hobby sat tight on the edge of the nest, peering up at the kestrel. The kestrel eased its way down through the canopy, edging along the branches towards the nest, whereupon the hobby flew at it aggressively, connecting this time, and forcing it out of the tree. When the two birds emerged they locked talons and both birds dropped down behind a hedge out of sight. The kestrel presumably flew off low across the field, since the hobby returned and perched near the nest a few minutes later, when the chicks became visible once more. A pair of kestrels nested in the adjacent field, but I assumed that the aggressive kestrel was not one of this pair, which I had seen in close proximity to the hobby nest several times without provoking a response.

The following stories did not reach the press but are nonetheless of interest.

## Fostering and production line

The lesser kestrel has sadly decreased in Europe over the past few decades and, in response, the Wildlife Service in Catalonia (northeastern Spain) implemented a recovery programme using captive birds from different parts of the country. The common kestrel played a pivotal role in the process carried out by Manuel Pomarol and his team.

Lesser kestrels are more difficult to breed in captivity than the common kestrel, as the former can be very nervous when incubating eggs and careless in rearing young. Only those lesser kestrel pairs that have proved themselves capable of completing the cycle successfully, having incubated common kestrel eggs and reared the chicks, are allowed to rear their own.

The captive common kestrel pairs were able to incubate other raptors' eggs including those of the lesser kestrel and Montagu's harrier, and to rear 20–25 chicks in a season, in similar-aged groups of no more than 10–12 chicks. After hatching in the laboratory, each group of birds was left with the foster pair when they were 5–10 days old and were taken out at 20–25 days. Once a group of chicks had been removed for release, another batch was put on the nest to continue the process.

The foster kestrels were carefully monitored, as even experienced birds can react adversely and may kill the young. This was extremely rare and most pairs were used only once in a season, because, in Manuel's words, they become 'more tired and careless'. In four years, the core three pairs of kestrels reared 90 common kestrels, 60 lesser kestrels and six Montagu's harrier chicks, a remarkable achievement.

Ideally, it is better for the lesser kestrel and Montagu's harriers to rear their own offspring and, as the years went by and the number of good parents increased, the load was taken off the common kestrels. Encouragingly, some of the released lesser kestrel chicks have returned to the area and are breeding successfully.

Apart from the captive breeding, cross-fostering also took place, with lesser kestrel chicks being exchanged for common kestrel in wild breeding pairs. This also proved successful.

## Kestrel Press

I had used Kestrel Press on several occasions in my work at Culzean Country Park so they were an obvious choice when a printer was needed for the 2009 Raptor Research Foundation Conference which was, for the first time, being held outside the USA, in Pitlochry, Scotland. When I went to collect the programmes in Irvine, the glass front of the building was boarded up, the result of an attempted ram raid. Access was round the side of the building and I immediately noticed a mass of kestrel droppings and pellets along the base of the wall. The girders above were obviously favoured by kestrels as a roosting site. When I mentioned this to the staff, they acknowledged that they had wondered about 'the mess' and were naturally delighted that a namesake was using their building. A nest box is being put up on the end of the building for the 2010 season.

*One of the Ayrshire kestrels made*
*famous by a local print firm*

Kestrel Press

### Drinks with the kestrel

I received an email from a Derek Burleigh in Majorca asking if I would like some pictures of a kestrel pair nesting in the wall of his house. The birds were confident and unperturbed by people or the two family dogs. The pictures duly arrived and made me jealous. The nest was located in a hole in the masonry just off the balcony. Imagine sitting sipping your drinks in the evening to the backdrop not of a boring old sunset but of a kestrel feeding young! All four young successfully fledged.

Nest here

*The Burleighs' house in Majorca showing the nest site on the balcony*

*Confident kestrel arrives at the nest hole in full view of those enjoying the balcony*

### Rhiannon

Being a long-time fan of Fleetwood Mac, I went to a live concert in Glasgow in October 2009. Imagine my surprise when, halfway through the concert, Stevie Nicks, the solo female singer, announced that she had been staying at Turnberry Hotel in south Ayrshire and had that very day had a very special encounter with a kestrel. The bird was one of a collection of raptors kept by the resident falconer Jamie Dempsey, whom I had known since he was very young, his family being close neighbours. She dedicated her next song *Rhiannon* to Jamie, whom I later learned was in the front row. The bird had been unnamed and, on being asked, Stevie had called her Rhiannon. It was a special moment for Jamie and, hopefully, made another convert to the world of kestrels.

*Rhiannon, the female kestrel named by Stevie Nicks of Fleetwood Mac fame*

# 6

## *Kindred spirits*

As this book will already have made clear, there are many people who contribute in different ways to kestrel work. There are others, part of a small but committed group who specialise in monitoring and protecting other raptor species. Although we often do our fieldwork individually there is a group responsibility for collating the annual data, supporting bird of prey conservation in the face of anti-raptor pressure groups which advocate controlling numbers for their own narrow interests.

I enjoy nothing better than the odd day in the field in the company of raptor enthusiasts who are working on other species. The fieldwork is often quite different and a lot can be learned from other people's experiences. Ricky Gladwell is the South Strathclyde raptor study group's hen harrier specialist and spends his spare time tracking down this much maligned and persecuted bird, both in the breeding season and at winter roosts.

I well remember the first time I visited a communal roost in the southwest, accompanied by Angus Hogg and John Melrose. We were spellbound at the sight of 25 grey males, ringtail females and juveniles arriving in dribs and drabs at the roost site, hawking the area before dropping onto favoured patches in the marshy terrain. They spend the night on rough, trampled-down platforms of rushes and grasses. Their pre-roost activity always makes it difficult to achieve an exact count when so many birds are involved.

*Female hen harrier in full voice above the nest site*

Being so busy with kestrel work, I often only get time for other species at the end of the season or during the kestrel incubation period. My first real field day with hen harriers was in July 1992 when I'd arranged to accompany Ricky to a fairly remote part of Ayrshire in the hope of seeing wing-tagging of harrier broods. Lashing rain and a stiff breeze did not deter us and, as usual, the timing was critical – Ricky was free on the Sunday and the gamekeeper was happy to allow access then as our presence would not disturb his work on the day of rest.

The first territory was quite a distance from the car but the walk was easy, along well-worn sheep tracks around heather-clad hillsides. Kestrels in the air above a Scots pine clump set me up for the day but the sad sight of a massive hill plough ripping through good heather habitat brought me back to reality. After half an hour, we rounded a hill and sat down to scan the bankings opposite. Ricky re-identified the nest site using the sketch in his notebook, a necessary aid when working with ground nesters in featureless terrain. On cue, a female hen harrier appeared over the skyline and hunted the slopes, overflying the nest site but never showing any sign of dropping in.

The young should have been quite well developed by then as two had hatched and four more had been chipping three weeks earlier, on 5 July. We walked over but, just as we made our final approach, I picked up four quills, definitely from a nestling harrier, and my worst fears were confirmed as the very exposed platform in shallow heather was empty.

While Ricky dejectedly collected pellets for analysis, I combed the heather for any clues. When Ricky found a partially-eaten young male harrier on a sheep path, a predator became the prime suspect. Certainly the heather had not been trampled round the site and in the wet conditions of the past couple of days any human intrusion would have left its mark. The flesh was fresh enough for the killing to have taken place earlier that morning. It was a very sober walk back, even when the kestrel family put on a second show above the pines.

Site two was viewed through a torrent of rain coming down like stair rods. Wet weather gear was an irrelevancy in the face of the deluge but thankfully it wasn't cold. The birds had flown and if they were still in the vicinity they were clamped down and sheltering. The nest, in rushes, had a maze of runs coming off it and droppings where the young had waited for food to be brought in. Finding a nest site in waist-high vegetation like this must require patience of a high order.

On we went through the monsoon, across sodden forestry ground, to the background noise of boots being sucked reluctantly from the quagmire. It was a case of head down and plod. After an hour, the rain relented and up came a trio of fledged hen harriers to take advantage of the break and wing their way over the young conifers. It was a superb sight. We noted the wing tags and identified the brood. Pair number three had certainly done well and Ricky was a happier man.

He was even more buoyant when we arrived at territory four, only 400 metres away, when the female harrier took to the air, 'yikkering' loudly. No heroics from her, though: she settled down to a pattern of circling the nest at about 100 metres, occasionally landing on heather mounds. This behaviour was in complete contrast with that of many of the birds which had nested in earlier decades. I remember ducking and weaving as hens aggressively and noisily pressed home their attacks, making contact and drawing blood from unprotected heads. These birds, alas, have paid a high price for their bravado and only the ones that slip away survive persecution. By now, our brief respite from the weather was nearly over as the light faded and the rain raced towards us over the moor.

*Ricky Gladwell ringing a
large harrier chick*

Ricky quickly set up his gear – with an umbrella to shelter proceedings – and we virtually waded back into the rushes to find two well-grown youngsters in yet another rush-protected site. Despite the poor light, they were photographed in situ before we removed one for processing. It was the third site where we noticed carrion beetles, presumably attracted by the prey remains. In this case they were crawling over the young, much to Ricky's disgust.

Time was not on our side and we quickly weighed, ringed and measured the bird and fixed a red tag on the left wing and a yellow on the right. The process was repeated with the second bird – they were both females, according to the measurements – and they were returned to the relative shelter of the nest before the heavens opened yet again. We left quickly to allow the adult back in if she wanted to brood the chicks.

The dreadful conditions made us decide not to visit the last site and we reluctantly retreated from this incredibly high-density area – three nests within a kilometre and 11 chicks wing-tagged that year. Ricky had finally decided that two males were supporting three females, which was not unusual.

Perversely, the sun came out on the walk back and suddenly this bleak area had lesser redpolls, skylarks, meadow pipits and wood pigeons appearing from nowhere. The ground flora was exceptional and the soft mid-summer hues were accentuated by the wet conditions – bog asphodel, cross-leaved heath and the fragrance of bog myrtle. We shared a welcome cup of tea. As we walked back, a couple of harriers were spotted on the skyline, but before we could positively identify them, a squall came in and down went the birds.

Undaunted, we saw out the interruption and were rewarded with superb views of two birds quartering above the young conifers, calling to each other. It was a fitting end to the day as the female was positively identified as last year's hen which had successful bred again that year in territory two. She was accompanied by one of her offspring, a female with the yellow and red combination, as opposed to the double yellow of the adult. The tags were very effective and easily recorded. They had moved further uphill from the natal site to much drier ground. Just to cap the day, a hen kestrel came into view and hovered, as usual, just out of camera range.

Back at the car the sodden clothing was peeled off: my feet resembled albino prunes. Another cup of tea, a family of four kestrels on the lower slopes and we were off home, knowing that our joints would be very painful for the next couple of days, a testimony to the years of amateur football we'd both played.

Ricky's figures for that year were very encouraging, with 17 pairs fledging 60 young. Forty four chicks were tagged and seven of the breeding females were already tagged, showing an improved survival rate. These females included one from Perthshire and another from Argyll.

It was a far cry from what had gone before. *The Birds of Ayrshire*, published in 1929, shows that, according to Lord Ailsa's gamekeepers' vermin list, 310 ash-coloured hawks were destroyed between 25 June 1850 and 25 November 1854. It is fair to say that the bird was unwelcome and paid a heavy price over the next hundred years. In 1960 three young harriers hatched at a nesting territory in Ayrshire, probably the first breeding record in the county this century. The colonisation has been painfully slow, due mainly to persecution. In 1984, for example, eight of the ten nesting attempts failed and only five young fledged from 43 eggs. The cause of failure was man.

Sadly, the persecution has continued virtually unabated and the productivity we witnessed on that damp July day is not the norm. It must be extremely depressing for Ricky to turn up at nest after nest to find anticipated broods absent and obvious telltale signs of human activity pinpointing the cause. Can you imagine how he felt in 2000 when, in his patch of 25 pairs attempting to breed, only two were successful? Even more disturbing were his failure figures, showing that the harrier is attracted to these territories year after year and that they are acting as a sump, sucking in potentially productive pairs only to have their breeding attempts wiped out. One can only imagine the destruction in 2001 when, with foot and mouth access restrictions in place, there was very limited monitoring, giving a virtual free hand to the anti-harrier brigade.

Anti-harrier feeling is so great in some quarters that Ricky has actually been threatened on several occasions. There seemed to be light at the end of the tunnel with the establishment of two Special Protection Areas for hen harriers in Ayrshire and in Dumfries and Galloway, but the reality is that in one of the areas, Muirkirk and North Lowther, the culture is so deeply ingrained that, despite the protective designation and the limiting of grouse shooting, harriers are still severely persecuted.

In the 1990s, the area supported 29 breeding females as part of one of the largest populations in Britain. By 2004, the number of breeding pairs dropped to 21, while the number of fledged young plummeted from 44 in that year to just five in 2008. In 2009, the number of pairs was down to 15 with only 13 young fledged from five nests, a slight improvement but still poor. One of the young was leucistic and probably had a life expectancy of zero. In the area of the SPA which I check, I did not see a single harrier that season.

Thankfully, the picture is not universally dire. The Isle of Arran, which has no persecution problems, has a thriving population while the Dumfries and West Galloway site where I've worked for the past four seasons has only one section which suffers. The contrast between the northern end of the SPA and the rest is stark. Virtually no birds breed in the north while there has been great success in the south, where any failures are associated with natural causes such as predation by foxes, poor weather and food shortages rather than human interference.

There is a marked contrast between working with a ground-nesting raptor and the kestrel and I was able to learn a great deal from Charlie Park and Geoff Sheppard when I began working on the SPAs. Cold searches are simply not an option on uniform moorland: it is the waiting game that counts and it is usually a game well worth playing. For sheer aerial acrobatic artistry, the cock hen harrier's sky-dancing display is one of the great bird experiences to watch. As if on a huge elastic band, it hurtles straight down at speed almost to ground level then swings back up, repeating this classic manoeuvre time after time. It's much easier to pinpoint the potential site if an unattached male lands frequently in the same place. 'Cock nests' can be built by the male and may be used later as a nest or roost.

*A 'cock nest' built by the male harrier but not chosen as the nesting site*

*A swab being taken to extract DNA to build up a population profile*

As if this spectacular display were not enough, the food pass is exquisite. This is one of the critical moments in locating the nest. As the hen is called off by the incoming male, she takes the prey in midair, talons outstretched. All attention must be on the hen as she does not always head back to the nest but will land and eat the prey item, sometimes quite a distance from the site. Real concentration is called for as she returns to the nest and drops out of sight. Even then, what you perceive at a distance in this featureless habitat can bear little resemblance to what you find when you finally arrive. A search of the area may still be required although the field has been narrowed considerably. Drawing a rough map from the vantage point can pay dividends later.

Even returning to check on the young can be exasperating, although GPS has helped, and the telltale down on the heather tips is a giveaway. The hen's behaviour, as explained earlier, has changed over the years and mock attacks have in most cases replaced full-blooded contact. Many hens just circle noisily at a distance. An empty nest can be misleading as the young are quite adventurous as they get older and, as a good survival technique, they move away from the nest platform and hide themselves away from the others in the surrounding cover.

After day 20, the young can be sexed by taking certain measurements. If the open claws measure less than 60 millimetres from point to point, the bird is likely to be a male, while a measurement of more than 62 millimetres indicates a female. If the leg can move freely in the slot for D rings on the ringing pliers, then the bird is a male, and if the bird weighs less than 400 grams, then it is also likely to be male. A weight of more than 450 grams confirms a female. Once the chicks are well-feathered, the male has a grey tinge to the iris while the female has a brown tinge. It's so much clearer than sexing kestrels in the nest.

A relatively recent development is the taking of a swab from inside the mouth of the nestlings to establish a DNA profile. This simple task is much easier than taking blood samples. The specimen is sealed and sent off for analysis, to be used to build up a database of individuals in the hard-pressed national population.

As we returned from a nest one day, we disturbed a short-eared owl from a small banking. Lying on a well-used grassy platform among the pellets and prey remains was a pure black short-tailed field vole, a first for both Geoff and me, after seeing literally thousands of normal-coloured individuals in nest boxes over the years.

*The vacated roost platform contained a black field vole as well as pellets and droppings*

In the southwest of Scotland we are very fortunate to have a strong population of barn owls and two Geoffs who monitor them. Both stalwarts of the Dumfries and Galloway raptor study group, and previously mentioned for their forestry work and hen harrier work respectively, Geoff Shaw and Geoff Sheppard have carried out long-term studies with impressive data sets going back decades. The fieldwork is again quite different from my work, with a largely sedentary population compared with the semi-nomadic kestrel, and adults which are relatively easily caught at nest sites which are usually accessible. A long breeding season also eases the time pressures. Barn owl fieldworkers work hard and are very committed, of course, but the numbers they can process are very significant and data on adults' mortality, turnover at nest sites and recruitment into the breeding population is easier to obtain for barn owls compared to the kestrels.

As the kestrel and barn owl often nest in similar nesting territories, occasionally using the same tree, buildings or quarries, and are both affected by the vole supply, I have worked closely with both the Geoffs. My first day out with Geoff Shaw in his study area in the Galloway Forest Park in April 1993 showed me just how difficult barn owl fieldwork can be.

Due to the scarcity of nest sites within the conifer monoculture, plastic barrels had been erected in trees to encourage the barn owl to breed. The aim was to check 16 territories during the day. In kestrel terms that was fairly ambitious but, as I was to find out, with the barn owl this was perfectly achievable.

We had a dry, dusty drive along forest roads but the company was good. It didn't take me long to become extremely envious of the ease with which information was collected without a great deal of physical effort. In conversation, it emerged that Geoff can predict as early as January which territories will be occupied by the sedentary barn owl, though not necessarily which birds will breed. The pace of the season is much more sedate than the frenetic, four-month blitz needed for kestrels. He can have barn owlets fledging as late as November. Handling the birds, too, is much less of a problem and as for checking nest boxes, the highest off the ground was 15 feet.

A single hen merlin basking in the mid-morning spring sunshine was our first bonus and the group of trees was carefully committed to memory for future inspection by Geoff. Under one of the sturdy bridges, a dipper dabbled in the peaty burn while on the specially-designed ledges below the main supports, old pied wagtail nests testified to the effectiveness of the design.

After a couple of blanks – empty barrels and no visible signs of owls – we parked the car at the edge of the forest at what Geoff described as one of the best bets. Net in hand, we moved along the line where sitka spruce met hill pasture until we reached the upright barrel lashed to a tree at a very comfortable height. On went the net, out came the cock and hen barn owl and that was that. Well, not quite. Both birds had to be extricated from the net, weighed and processed. Both birds were new to the territory; the hen's history was known, but the male was unringed. She was an older hen and sported very few spots on her chest, a characteristic of a mature bird. The sedentary barn owl is not prone to great movements and most of the ringing returns are local. The two beautiful specimens could hardly have been more docile, but we still gave the large talons due respect.

The second occupied territory was centred on an old steading within the forest, with so many escape routes that catching was almost impossible. Breeding hadn't started but both

*Left: Geoff Shaw with two adult barn owls caught in the same box*

*Below: The barn owl crouched and hissed when the barrel top was removed*

birds left one of the upper rooms. Lying in one of the corners were the remains of one of last year's young birds, identified by the ring which was still attached. The fact that the building was still roofed was critical, as the owls rarely use sites once cover has gone. Dozens of the owls' distinctive black pellets littered the floor and the copious whitewash was a good indicator of a well-used site.

Nest three, in a barrel, proved to be the furthest advanced, the hen sitting on four eggs. She was reluctant to leave and was caught in the barrel. Again, she was an older hen which had moved into what Geoff rated as a prime territory with good feeding, due to the more diverse hunting area at the edge of the forest. Even in bad vole years, this territory supported breeding pairs, two voles cached at the edge of the nest confirming this.

The picture was much as for the kestrel that year: prime sites occupied but with slow progress in terms of breeding. Three occupied territories out of 16 was little reward for seven hours in the field but I'd really enjoyed the day. It made a welcome change to be the one who held the birds, took down the notes, opened the gates and generally played second fiddle. A date was set for a return visit later in the season and on 25 August, well past the date when I'd be out with the kestrels, we set out again.

I met Geoff at the same rendezvous and we set out to check on the progress of the remaining five pairs which should still have had young in the nest. One the way in to the first pair we passed one forest territory which had been prospected by a kestrel hen in May. It eventually deposited an egg in the vertical barrel before deserting in the face of June's deluge. It was a surprise choice of nest site because of the degree of difficulty in exiting up the sides of the barrel. Owls are great scramblers, but kestrels tend to like a reasonably flat surface. I have seen only two other instances of kestrels in these barrels and the young were probably the dirtiest I've ever seen, restricted as they were to the base of the barrel and unable to keep clean. The small exit hole high in the barrel did not allow the passage of air or the opportunity to dry out after wet weather.

We closed in on the barrel where the pair of barn owls had been caught on the last visit and recaptured the hen. She was absolutely scruffy, her tail hardly recognizable, her facial disc smeared with dirt and her claws positively disgusting. To judge by her condition she must have been spending a lot of time in the box. Unusually, she was very aggressive, behaving much more like a tawny owl. Her two ten-day old chicks were in good condition but with the weather so unpredictable, the odds were not in their favour. They would probably fledge in October, leaving little time to build up resources and experience before life got tough in the winter.

Geoff took me on a slight detour into a stand of larch in the forest to check another barrel which had housed rather special residents earlier in the year. The trunk of the tree was badly scarred with claw marks and the lid was completely covered with smelly grey droppings. It was the breeding den of a pine marten pair which Geoff had found, and they were using the top of the barrel as a latrine. The female had stayed in the box with her three kits and did not seem to mind the disturbance. In the early 1980s the Forestry Commission released martens into the Galloway Forest Park where they have not only survived but prospered. From 1988 onwards it became clear that the pine martens were using large-sized nest boxes on trees, which were intended for owls, as winter dens. There were no martens present that day, the latrine had no fresh scats but the inside of the barrel had a two-inch lining of dead bees. Presumably they had chosen the wrong location and had perished en masse on an evening when the combination of low temperatures and the poor insulation of a plastic box had proved fatal.

The next two nest sites were in A-frame boxes which, though more time-consuming to make, had the great advantage of wood as a material and a roomy base. In each case immaculate juvenile barn owls emerged, having chosen to roost in the boxes while the rest of the broods preferred the nearby trees.

We were definitely on a roll and in the next barrel, all three young had survived. The aggressive male chick flung itself at Geoff as he peered beneath the lid, while its two docile female nestmates lay back and swayed in unison. There were about 50 days old and had to be handled carefully to keep their wayward lashing claws from damaging themselves or the other nestlings. One female bird had a peach-coloured breast, which occurs occasionally in barn owls.

At the last site, the hen came off three newly-hatched owlets. It was hard to believe hatching at such a late date. She was an old bird and unringed so one, at least, had slipped through the net. In reality this meant that Geoff would not be able to finish his season and calculate his figures until the middle of October, a full three months after the last kestrel had flown. The pace of his season has a lot to commend itself.

One of the great fascinations to me in raptor work is the comparative responses of the barn owl and kestrel to vole cycles. The voles in southwest Scotland typically build up to a peak level of abundance every three years, followed by a collapse in numbers and subsequent recovery to the next peak. Both species therefore experience large variations in their preferred prey from year to year, and the breeding strategies they adopt could not be more different. Combining Geoff's data and my own for the period 1985 to 2000 (Shaw and Riddle 2003) highlights the responses of one diurnal and one nocturnal predator to the same food supply.

Both species showed considerable variation in breeding numbers from year to year but each followed an approximate three-year cycle. There was, however, a contrasting pattern for each species, barn owl numbers tending to reach a peak in the year following a good vole year, and declining the next season. Kestrel numbers peaked in the good vole year and always declined steadily the following year.

*Annual mean clutch size of Kestrel in south-west Scotland study area 1985–2009 (arrows = vole years)*

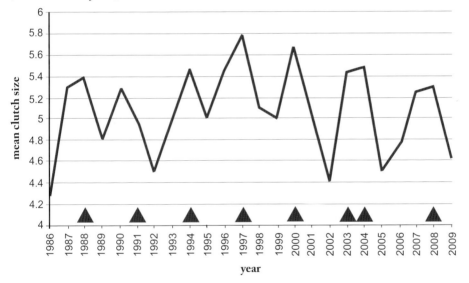

Overall the barn owl breeding performance showed a stronger association with annual trends in field vole numbers. Although both species bred earlier and produced more eggs in peak vole years, only the owls exhibited extreme fluctuations in productivity that matched vole cycles. Following a collapse in vole numbers, many barn owls did not breed at all, while those that did laid small clutches late in the season with productivity very low. Most kestrels in the study area laid eggs every year and reared young even in those years when the owls were least productive.

The barn owl was much more dependant on field voles than was the kestrel, which was able to switch to other prey when necessary. Barn owl diet was typically 70–80 % voles, while the kestrel diet was dominated by field voles when they were numerous. Other small mammals, birds, lizards and invertebrates featured predominantly in other years. Kestrels appeared to behave as vole specialists when conditions were right but became generalists, switching to alternative prey, when voles were scarce.

Ringing recoveries demonstrated that barn owls were resident in the study area, with territories occupied all year round. As a result, barn owls always started to breed earlier than kestrels when vole numbers were high. In such years up to 20% of pairs reared a second brood, with young leaving the nest as late as November. As largely nocturnal hunters, barn owls could maximize their foraging time by extending their breeding season before and after the period of maximum day length. Although barn owl productivity was depressed every third year, the birds were able to respond rapidly to increase chick production when conditions were good.

The more mobile kestrel was found to disperse to winter in southern Britain and northern Europe and returning birds had more flexibility in selecting areas when food sources were sufficient to support a breeding attempt. However, the breeding season was restricted to a single brood and few clutches were started after May. As diurnal predators, kestrels are constrained to a period of greatest day length to meet the foraging demand of a brood. Nevertheless, in general, productivity was higher for kestrels but this may be balanced by the extra risks involved in migration and the need to secure a territory each year.

Both strategies seem to be successful as the southwest of Scotland has strong populations of both species.

In Geoff Sheppard's study areas in west Galloway, the majority of barn owls nest in buildings. Due to the upsurge of second or holiday homes in this popular area, the loss of nest sites as old deserted farm buildings and remote cottages are upgraded or converted has become a problem. However, Geoff has compensated for this by putting up a large number of nest boxes on beams, on outhouses and, if possible, on new buildings. The nest boxes in those sheltered sites can become very warm in the summer months and, on opening boxes to retrieve young for ringing, the smell of ammonia can knock you back

*Geoff Sheppard returning a young barn owl to the nest box after ringing*

*As the owlets grew, space in the barrel was at a premium*

*A healthy brood of barns owls in my old hide in the Dam*

Most people are delighted to have barn owls as neighbours and Geoff keeps them well informed as the breeding season progresses. The young birds are particularly photogenic. Their comical appearance, with the down feathers on their heads making them look like punks or lawyers wearing wigs, and their fantastic facial discs make them ideal subjects for study. Their odd habit of swaying and their repertoire of hisses and snores add enormously to their appeal. Their ability to remove rodents, especially rats, from the vicinity of buildings is also appreciated by their hosts. Like the kestrel, the barn owl enjoys very good public relations.

Geoff's study goes back a quarter of a century and he monitors 70–80 pairs annually. His main work revolves round the age structure of the population, catching an impressive 80–100 adults each year and ringing a further 100–200 young, depending upon the prevailing conditions. His birds really don't move far, the males on average nine kilometres and the females 23. Kestrels do on occasion nest very close to his barn owls, one pair having their nest against the barn owl nest box. Few kestrels use the barn owl-type boxes but feral pigeons do, and have on a number of occasions shared the box with the owls and reared young.

For years I avidly followed the fortunes of the precarious remnant population of red kites in Welsh valleys as this once-widespread bird struggled to retain a toehold in Britain. I looked at the pictures, read the papers and articles, watched the television programmes and even ventured south to see some birds in flight, but it was all distant stuff.

A reintroduction scheme had seen young birds released in several areas of Scotland and England and now it was the turn of Dumfries and Galloway. The year 2001 saw the first release of kites there, in the face of severe problems associated with the foot and mouth outbreak. Thirty three birds were released, the number boosted by a contingent from Germany which had been intercepted as part of an investigation into the illegal trafficking of birds of prey. The birds were offered to Scotland and gladly received in an excellent example of European conservation co-operation.

Partnerships have been a key factor in the successful release programmes: government agencies such as Scottish Natural Heritage and English Nature have worked closely with the Royal Society for the Protection of Birds, raptor study groups, local landowners and farmers.

In Scotland these releases have been in the Inverness area, in central Scotland, Galloway and on the outskirts of Aberdeen.

On 22 July 2002 I drove down to Dumfries and Galloway at the invitation of Chris Rollie to see red kites at very close quarters. Geoff Shaw and I had previously travelled up to the Doune release site in central Scotland to see the set-up and to watch released birds coming in to a communal woodland roost. In 2001, during the foot and mouth outbreak, I had visited the Galloway release cages but now, with any luck, I was to see birds at very close quarters. A team was due to fit some of that year's cohort with radio transmitters and wing tags to facilitate monitoring after release.

*Chris Rollie at the first set of release cages in Galloway*

The drive down was typical of the dreadful summer, with our headlights still on at 9 a.m., but, thankfully, the weather had relented by the time I reached Kevin Duffy's house and the sun had even broken through. The team which gathered for a welcome cup of tea could not have been more experienced in the kite field: Duncan Orr-Ewing and Brian Etheridge, veterans of the Scottish release programme.

The 24 birds in that year's batch were in three sets of release pens in three discrete locations, each with eight birds in residence. The sites were well spread out to minimize even the remote possibility of disease causing a problem. The drive to the first site was through typical red kite habitat, open mixed farmland with scattered mature woodland and rolling low-lying ridges, rather than the steep valleys of the Welsh remnant population.

Arriving at the first release point, we unloaded the equipment, an interesting mix of the expected – radio transmitters and wing tags, and the unexpected – four folding chairs, rubber tubing, dental floss, superglue and needles. The birds were housed in spacious pens designed to allow observation and feeding through spyholes and feed gloves without the need for human contact. An exception was made only if emergency veterinary treatment was needed. The birds viewed their world through the wire frontage, never seeing Kevin as he carried out his daily checking and feeding, and never becoming imprinted.

We soon settled down to a standard routine, Kevin, Duncan and Brian processing each bird with Katie, from another release area, and me acting as willing gofers, collecting and returning the birds to the cages and handing over pieces of equipment as requested. The birds themselves

*Left: Red kite viewed through the inspection spyhole*

*Below: Feeding carried out using a glove system to minimise imprinting of the birds*

were stunningly beautiful and, once caught, were incredibly docile in the hand, making little or no attempt to escape. Kestrels of the same age would never have stopped trying to rip you apart. One endearing trait was that the birds would slowly bend their heads forward in a bowed position, as if resigning themselves to being handled. That is not to say that their behaviour was faultless, with Duncan receiving a nasty puncture from a wayward talon.

What impressed me most was the meticulous care taken in fitting the transmitters, a very fiddly job. The strongest tail feather, usually the central one, was selected and the transmitter, attached to a small piece of rubber tube, was carefully slid down the feather vane and into position. The barbs were teased out and repositioned. The aerial was then tied onto the vane at several points using dental floss, and superglued to make doubly sure that it was secure. The ends of the dental floss were then cut off and, when the glue was dry, the final professional touch was to use a marker pen to darken the tiny glue spots. The process was slow and the birds' welfare was always taken into consideration. Meanwhile, the captive human prey watching from the seats were assaulted by a very determined and typically Scottish team of midges, flies and cleggs.

Each bird was wing-tagged and then weighed by simply laying them on the scales, Any bird weighing in at over 1,100 grams was sexed as a definite female and there was a high percentage in the batch. Naturally, Brian claimed that the heaviest and healthiest were the birds donated from the Inverness area. All the birds were, in fact, in excellent condition, all good weights and with surprisingly little feather damage to wings, tails or ceres from their confinement in cages. The cages themselves were pretty smelly by this time and must have resembled natural nests, with prey remains littering the area below the platforms and the associated crowds of flies.

There was lots of banter, and serious discussion too, as the work progressed, taking in subjects like the pros and cons of using lightweight harnesses and backpack radio transmitters which last longer but which may have a detrimental effect on the survival of the bird. The transmitters on the tail feathers function only until the next moult, giving a very limited window of opportunity for the supply of data. The following year, backpacks were used and have not in fact proved to be a major problem.

Another talking point was the future of the programmes, given that an incredible one third of red kites released in Scotland have perished, mostly due to poisoning. Sadly, some of the Galloway releases have already succumbed and the sooner the practice is stamped out the better, for the countryside in general and the red kite in particular.

Another, very special invitation came in 2003, to the release of that year's kites. Eleven birds in total had been housed in the cages and took less than ten minutes to set free. The release cages were opened by lowering one of the hinged front sections, forming a platform to assist the first flight. They all exited differently: some came out flying hard and never touched the

136

*Kestrels for Company*

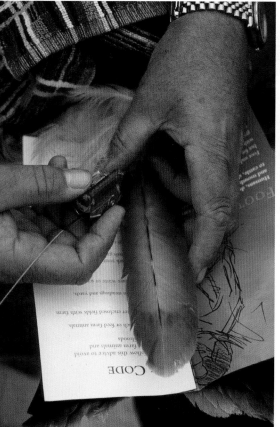

*Above: Wing tags indicating the year and the release area*

*Left: Fixing the transmitter to the tail feather*

*Clockwise from top left: The red kite team – Duncan Orr-Ewing,*
*Brian Etheridge, Duncan Cameron and Kevin Duffy*

*George Christie, Red Kite Project Officer for Dumfries and Galloway, opens the release cages*

*Some come out tentatively, others like rockets*

platform, others sat bemused at the edge, while the rest landed on the cage roof before psyching themselves up for the dash to freedom.

As might be expected, they were very clumsy in takeoff, but they had to get their act together quickly in order to gain height and clear the trees which fringed the clearing. Only one stayed in the vicinity and a few of us did a circuit to flush it back into the clearing and away. It was a brief experience but will live long in the memory for the group of enthusiasts who had been involved in the project. Kevin later checked the radio telemetry to confirm that all the birds were safe. After the initial scattering, they would meet up quickly, associate with adults, meet at feed dumps and even come back to the cages where food was left out for some time.

Kevin has now moved on and so has the project. George Christie is the current Red Kite officer and the population in 2010 now stands at 51 laying pairs which produced 98 young. A total of 104 red kites were released up to 2005. The population is now established and is expanding year on year, with the Red Kite Trail now part of the local tourist scheme. At the feeding station these masters of flight can be viewed at close quarters and on my last visit there were almost a hundred birds in the air. It was a stunning sight and Chris and his team have done a great job.

*Invaluable radio telemetry allows the birds to be monitored*

158    *Magnificent red kites flying again in Galloway*

With the Aberdeen project now up and running, there is little likelihood of further release programmes in Scotland. In 2009, the population of red kites there reached a 150-year high, with 149 pairs fledging 234 young. Problems still exist with persecution and poisoning, especially in the area around the first release point north of Inverness, but the return of the red kite to our avian fauna through the reintroduction scheme of the last 20 years can only be regarded as a huge success story.

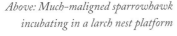
*Above: Much-maligned sparrowhawk incubating in a larch nest platform*

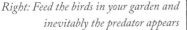
*Right: Feed the birds in your garden and inevitably the predator appears*

I have only highlighted three species to give a flavour of the different types of fieldwork being carried out. There is much more happening in our area, such as Ian Todd's work on the sparrowhawk. For a long time Ian, from the South Strathclyde Raptor Study Group, ploughed a lone furrow and there was little coverage of this species in Scotland despite Ian Newton's groundbreaking work in Dumfries and Galloway. A comprehensive programme of work is now ongoing in Edinburgh, however, with excellent comparative data from Mike McGrady's monitoring of the urban population between 1986 and 1989.

The peregrine is also monitored closely by a large team of enthusiasts co-ordinated by Chris Rollie. In 2009, the peregrine in the southwest of Scotland had its worst year since 2002 in terms of chick production. There is still a stark contract in terms of occupancy rates and productivity between grouse moor areas and adjacent sites, suggesting that persecution is a major issue in the former. It's a good example of the value of long-term work being carried out by raptor workers to assess accurate trends.

Kindred Spirits
Tumbling, cronking raw raven dawn
Scavenging rogues engaging the air
Rolling, coasting, effortless free fall
Sheer joy and gymnastics
Blatant exhibitionists, reprobates all.
Teasing black silver sheen
An unkindness or murder collective
At ease on the hill
Honorary raptor.

Bold, dashing, hugging the contour
Much maligned victim of dinosaur mindsets
Struggling to prosper in a place they should grace
Skydancer supreme, the moorland performer
Romancing the wind
Talons outstretched, an intimate passing
The bond secure, a harrier moment.

Pocket power at pace
Jack Russell of the raptor world
Smallest of the genre with attitude
Tailgater, demon chaser
Master of the lower air space
Dash and catch, the merlin.

Kettles of buzzards boiling once more
The long lazy glide over ancestral haunts
A title hard won, now commonest of all
This very success could come at a price
Not everyone welcomes the mews overhead.

Surgical instruments strike at great speed
Hit and run expert designed for surprise
A weaver and jinker could play on the wing
Fleeting glimpse of sparrowhawk flair
Master of the wood and edge.

The author of ghost stories
Snores, hisses and shrieks
Quartering silently hawking the sward
Then veers and drops deadly
Intent on the task
The lightweight assassin, a few moments gone
The barn owl rises with talons tight.

For years on Welsh precipice
New lease of life
Flock feeding spectacular, public delight
At home in good company, a social affair
Still someway to go, the few spoil the journey
Kites flying again, kindred spirits.

# 7

## *Reflections*

Thirty nine unbroken seasons in the company of kestrels. My aspirations in 1972 never came within a mile of this, especially in relation to the way I have put down roots and completed a third of a century monitoring in one locality. In retrospect, I would change neither the sojourn in this corner of southwest Scotland nor the choice of raptor. The kestrel, though, cannot be viewed in isolation: it is part of a wider raptor story. This is an opportune moment, in the first years of the new millennium, to reflect on what has been a period of tangible progress in the field of raptor conservation. Certainly most populations are in a healthier state today compared to the lows of the late 1960s and early 1970s when I became seriously involved with the kestrel work.

Make no mistake, it has been anything but plain sailing, and the long haul back for some of our birds of prey is by no means over. The substantial increase in what we know about them and the positive measures taken to protect them have unfortunately been countered by continual widespread persecution and habitat mismanagement by certain elements in the countryside. This has kept the brakes firmly on progress. The net result is that, despite some improvements in range and numbers, the majority of bird of prey species are still far short of the population levels which the country could support. You only have to travel in certain parts of continental Europe to see what is possible, while here in the United Kingdom, many raptors are still very much in recovery mode.

A trawl of the articles and papers published around 1972, when I first became involved in this field, confirms early memories of a fragile situation. Although raptors were slowly recovering from the lows of pesticide-induced population reductions in the 1950s and 1960s, the general consensus was that if another major setback were to occur, the consequences would be catastrophic, given the small sizes of core populations.

Although much of what follows does take in the UK dimension, there is obviously a Scottish and personal bias, given that my perspective is influenced by my fieldwork and experience here in Scotland. There have been a series of ups and downs in the now well-documented relationship between raptors and man in the past two centuries. By 1916, persecution on a grand scale had eliminated the marsh harrier, goshawk, white-tailed sea eagle, honey buzzard and osprey as breeding birds in Britain, while the egg-and skin collectors hammered the last nails in the coffin. To put these losses into perspective, these are five of the 15 species currently breeding in the United Kingdom.

*The sea eagle is aptly nicknamed 'the flying barn door'*

Many other populations were much reduced in number due to the blanket status of 'vermin' afforded them by the owners and managers of the large sporting estates created in the 19th century. The sump effect of persecution in these game-rearing areas caused a debilitating drain on raptor numbers. Breeding pairs were removed annually from nesting territories, resulting in a failure to produce young, and the loss was often compounded by the killing of non-breeding birds attracted to those prime sites when the original pair had been destroyed. It was a far cry from the elevated status and close working relationships with man enjoyed by some raptors during the falconry period in the Middle Ages, before the invention of the modern firearm and its application to game sports. In a relatively short time, raptors went from ally to outcast.

Respites during the two world wars, when many gamekeepers were on military service, allowed some populations to rebuild, although peregrine falcons on the south coast of England fared badly. During the period 1939–1945, more than 600 were officially killed to prevent the loss of carrier pigeons which were being used for communication during times of radio silence, or to bring home news of downed Allied aircraft over occupied Europe. Persecution did resume between 1918 and 1939 and after 1945 but gamekeeper numbers were beginning to decline as many estates broke up due to the considerable change in the socio-economic climate of Britain.

The panacea of pesticides as the answer to the control of agricultural pests after 1945 proved to be a false dawn when disastrous side effects were identified in the environment. Ironically, it was complaints by pigeon fanciers about excessive peregrine numbers that highlighted the problems. In fact, the opposite turned out to be true and, after much fieldwork, analysis and lobbying, voluntary and legal bans on the use of these chemicals eventually began to halt the serious downward trends in peregrine numbers.

*Coastal peregrine, the victim of pesticide poisoning*

It is worth looking at the status of some of the key species and comparing their situation in 1972 with today's figures to gain an insight into the tremendous progress that has been made. The peregrine falcon had been particularly affected by pesticides, preying as it does upon grain-eaters such as pigeons which accumulated persistent organochlorines from seed dressings. The 1930 UK figure of 1,100 pairs had slumped to 360 in 1963, of which fewer than 150 produced young. The national census of 1971 recorded 341 territories occupied by pairs or single birds, 80% of which were in Scotland. Adult mortality had slowed down but the output of fledged young was poor. Dr Derek Ratcliffe, who co-ordinated the survey and later wrote a monograph on the species (Ratcliffe 1980) stated that the population was delicately balanced. He was also instrumental in proving the link between pesticides and the egg-shell thinning that was partly driving the declines.

A decade later and another national survey revealed an encouraging climb to over 700 pairs, which increased to 1,285 pairs occupying nesting territories in UK in 1991, of which half were in Scotland. However, the picture was not uniformly rosy. In coastal and inland areas of the northern Highlands, numbers had declined since 1981, with contamination by marine pollutants in seabird prey probably playing a part (Crick *et al.* 1995).

The most recent survey in 2002 estimated that 1514 peregrine territories were occupied by pairs or single birds, plus an estimated occupation of territories which were not visited. This showed an encouraging 11% increase from 1991 and a remarkable 63% increase from 1930 (Banks *et al.* 2003). Geographical differences did emerge, with rapid expansion in the south of England offset by declines in northern Scotland. The reasons put forward for the increase were a range expansion due to a healthy food supply, possibly a greater tolerance of human activity and changes in the use of pesticides. Declines were attributed to a combination of factors, including the inevitable persecution. Overall it suggests a much healthier state of affairs than in 1972 but vigilance is still needed. The population of peregrines in southwest Scotland in 2009 was down from a high of 80 pairs in 1996 and 1997 to 52 pairs. The decline is almost exclusively made up of inland territories and as there is no decrease in productivity, persecution is probably the main factor. Significantly, inland territories have increased in south Strathclyde, the sites being in inaccessible buildings or secure quarries.

*Merlins will utilise old crow's nests on moorland fringe*

The peregrine falcon story is now a classic example of how the combined efforts of the government, conservation bodies, industry and individuals, along with the application of public pressure, have reversed a potential environmental disaster, and how vital raptors are as prime biological indicators at the top of the food chain.

Our smallest raptor, the merlin, was also badly affected by pesticides and had the dubious distinction of having even higher average levels of pesticide in victims than the sparrowhawk and peregrine. However, the merlin story is slightly different, in that declines had been noted before the pesticide era, due probably to a combination of persecution and loss or deterioration of moorland habitat. Ironically, merlins, which nest predominantly on the ground in the United Kingdom, are more productive on keepered ground if unmolested by man, as mammalian predators such as foxes and stoats which prey on sitting adults, eggs and young, are controlled.

The low point in merlin population numbers was in the 1950s and 1960s when the number of pairs was estimated at around 550. The merlin was certainly a rare sight in Ayrshire in the early 1970s. A national survey in 1983–1984 produced an estimate of 550–650 pairs and the follow-up survey a decade later indicated a much healthier position of 1,300 pairs (Rebecca and Bainbridge, 1998). Care must be taken when making direct comparisons as coverage was much better in the second survey, but certainly a moderate recovery had taken place.

The 2008 survey concluded that the population was relatively stable at around 1,140 breeding pairs in the UK but, as with the peregrine, some declines were identified in certain regions, for example in south Scotland. More survey work and analysis is needed to determine the factors causing those declines.

The golden eagle, too, has shown an upward trend from around 250–300 pairs in 1972 to 420 pairs in surveys carried out in 1982 and 1992 respectively (Green 1996) although there were some shifts in distribution. The 2003 survey (Eaton *et al.*) put the number of occupied territories at approximately 440. A huge expansion is not expected but realistically this bird has the potential to reach 500 pairs in Scotland, similar to the population in 1900. The golden eagle is a long-lived slow breeder with relatively low productivity compared with smaller raptors, and it does not have the capacity to recover quickly. Current factors which affect it – persecution, loss of hunting habitat due to blanket afforestation, over-grazing, egg collecting and human disturbance – add up to a formidable raft of obstacles to further expansion south of the border into former haunts (50 pairs bred in England and Wales pre-1900). In Scotland, there are still significant areas of suitable habitat where golden eagle fail to breed.

*What better sight than a golden eagle in full flight?*

In *The Conservation Framework for the Golden Eagle*, Whitfield *et al.* (2008) identified 'unexpected gaps' in eagle population areas and poor breeding results, attributing these to persecution. This was particularly noticeable in the central and eastern Highlands and in upland areas south of the Highlands, where moorland is managed for the shooting of red grouse.

The staggering statistic is that there are 250 vacant territories. The correlation between poor territory occupation and low production of young, and driven grouse moor management, indicates strongly that illegal persecution is affecting the conservation status of golden eagles, providing scientific confirmation of what eagle workers have known for many years. In other areas where poor breeding was identified, the causes were attributed to a contribution of heavy grazing by sheep and deer and the burning of vegetation.

Another species which can be bracketed in the 'slow to expand' section is the osprey, a classic exemplar in the British raptor conservation field. Extinct in 1916, there were various breeding attempts until a single pair, probably emanating from Scandinavia, nested in the Spey Valley in 1954. The decision by the Royal Society for the Protection of Birds to open the doors to the public and provide facilities for viewing the breeding site was as imaginative as it was brave and richly deserved the success that followed. The repercussions of this will be discussed later in the chapter. As a trainee ranger naturalist, I remember being shown the protective methods being used at the site on a visit with Roy Dennis in 1971 and I still possess a memento, a stick from below the nest which had been broken off a tree by an osprey. Things have come a long way since then and the arrangements today are much more sophisticated.

By 1972 the recolonisation of the Speyside area was on course, with 12 territories occupied and six pairs rearing 15 young. The rarity status of the birds has always attracted the unwelcome attention of egg collectors and this mindless practice still haunts the species today. From the Strathspey nucleus, ospreys have expanded over much of the central Highlands of Scotland and the 1995 figures of 97 pairs rearing 142 young speak volumes for the efforts of many people. By 1998, numbers had reached 130 pairs and the new millennium saw breeding in England for the first time in over a century. Expansion is now progressing well with birds now breeding in southern Scotland and Cumbria, and overall numbers of breeding pairs exceed 200. Roy Dennis' book *A Life of Ospreys* (2008) is a must-read and pulls the whole story together.

Such is the progress being made by ospreys that between 1991 and 2001, a total of 64 young birds from the Scottish population were translocated to Rutland Water in England with some returning from Africa to first breed there in 2001. Now young Scottish ospreys are being translocated to Coto Doñana in southern Spain in an effort to re-establish breeding ospreys on the mainland, where the last pair bred in 1982. Could the pioneers of osprey conservation in the early 1950s have dreamed that this would happen?

Like the osprey, goshawks too had become extinct but their re-establishment as a breeding bird in Britain from the 1950s onwards was largely as a result of the deliberate release of birds

*146*  *Two young ospreys ready for transportation to Rutland Water*

by falconers or of accidental escapes. One theory is that around 250 birds made it into the wild by one means or another in the 1970s alone. In 1972, the situation in Scotland was by no means clear-cut, and although sightings had increased, no nests had been found (*Scottish Bird Report* 1972). This is not surprising as the bird is elusive and numbers must have been very small at that time. Today the British population stands at around 500 pairs while in Scotland, numbers are estimated at over 150 pairs (Marquess, M. in press) and increasing. Persecution is the main limiting factor as pheasants are well within the goshawk's prey range and toleration levels in game-rearing areas are very low.

One of the most astonishing comebacks has been made by the common buzzard. In addition to the usual setbacks of persecution and pesticides, the buzzard has also had to contend with the effects of myxomatosis in the 1950s when its main prey item, the rabbit, was decimated. A population of approximately 12,000 pairs in the early 1950s fell dramatically in 1957 following widespread myxomatosis then recovered to 8,000–10,000 pairs by 1970. I can remember small pockets of breeding birds in Ayrshire in the early 1970s but it was uncommon to see soaring birds, despite the availability of huge tracts of ideal habitat. The national survey in 1983 put numbers at 12,000–15,000 pairs and noted an extension of the bird's range, especially in southern England. East and northeast Scotland were the only exceptions, apparently due to persecution. As a carrion feeder, the buzzard is very susceptible to illegal poisoned bait and this extremely dangerous and indiscriminate method of eradication has in the past slowed down range expansion. Sadly, this practice is still prevalent in some areas. The expansion of the buzzard is very obvious locally and nowadays I certainly see buzzard virtually on a daily basis. It is once more a very welcome common breeding bird in Ayrshire.

*147*

*Not everyone welcomes the healthy expansion of the buzzard*

A recent paper by Rob Clements paints a very positive picture (Clements 2002). The buzzard in recent years has broken out from its western and northern strongholds and has spread eastwards. There is also evidence that it is breeding at a much higher density, especially in prey-rich farmland habitat. A reduction in persecution and an increase in the rabbit population are contributing causes in this healthy expansion. The new national population estimate suggests a level of about 44,000–61,000 territorial pairs in 2001, making the buzzard the most abundant diurnal raptor in Britain. Predictably, this has resulted in calls from the game-rearing lobby for licences to control buzzards where conflict with their business is proven. I can see this becoming yet another *cause célèbre*.

*Above: Rabbit on the menu for these buzzard chicks*

*Right: Female hen harrier in full voice while a brood was ringed*

In the winter of 2008–2009, there were a large number of reports of first-year buzzards in poor condition being handed in to animal rescue centres, or being found dead during a particularly severe spell of weather. What a difference it makes to be able to observe natural factors coming to the fore rather than persecution.

The hen harrier is one of the most spectacular and beautiful birds of prey to watch and it is fair to say that, of all raptor species, its presence is the most contentious, being perceived as public enemy number one on keepered ground. The descriptions 'rats with wings' or 'mink with wings' are often used by its detractors and sum up the perverse attitude in some quarters to this stunning bird.

Widespread throughout Britain pre-1900, it was restricted by the turn of the century to Orkney and the Western Isles of Scotland. The recolonisation of mainland Scotland began in the

*Healthy brood of harriers, the runt still surviving*

1930s and the bird successfully exploited the new forestry plantations of the 1960s and 1970s, in which they could breed relatively unmolested. By the 1970s, the population was put at 500–600 pairs and regrettably its status has not improved much over the three decades since then.

The first full national survey in 1988–1989 calculated 478–699 pairs, a figure not so different from the 570 territorial pairs found in the 1998 survey. The most recent population estimate following the 2004 survey showed a 41% increase in the UK and Isle of Man population to 806 territorial pairs (Sim *et al.* 2007). Once more, the picture was not consistent across the country. In Scotland, the Orkney population had picked up after a decline from the late 1970s (Amar *et al.* 2003) but there were declines in the east Highlands and southern uplands. Again a decrease was recorded on grouse moors. The preliminary results of the 2010 survey show a depressing reduction in pairs of 22% with a significant decline over all regions in Scotland.

Research work comparing the hen harrier's success on keepered, as distinct from unkeepered, ground highlighted the problem. Deliberate intensive persecution is still prevalent, just as it was nearly a century ago, and this is severely depressing numbers. In 2008, only five pairs of hen harriers successfully bred in all the prime habitat of Scottish driven grouse moors (Scottish Raptor Monitoring Group). Even Special Protection Area status has not slowed the persecution. In the Muirkirk and North Lowther Uplands SPA in south west Scotland, where 29 breeding females supported one of the largest populations in Britain in the 1990s, the number has now dropped to 14. Production of young has declined from 44 in 2004 to just five in 2008.

Once more the sump effect exacerbates the problem: prospective breeders are attracted to empty territories and in-fill, only to be killed themselves. Threats to winter roosts and the

*In the current persecution blitz, what chance does a white harrier have?*

targetted burning of heather at active nests add to the pressure. If the persecution does not stop, then the hen harrier stands little chance of extending its range to achieve the carrying capacity in suitable available habitat. In England the picture is even bleaker with only a remnant of 12 pairs hanging on despite suitable habitat being available for in excess of 300 pairs.

I could use the marsh harrier and sea eagle as other examples, but their stories would be similar: slow recovery following numerous reversals and a common limiting factor in man's activities. The exception is the aerobatic hobby, a summer visitor to Britain which is increasing with – at present – no apparent adverse factors.

We must not lose sight of the fact that there have been some very positive developments in the past four decades which together have greatly improved the lot of our birds of prey. There is every reason to be proud of the increases in species numbers and ranges and of the efforts of dedicated fieldworkers and conservation bodies, especially the RSPB. Several factors have been critical in building up this momentum, namely the development of an infrastructure to monitor raptors, advances in technology to aid this work, the positive cultural and economic impact of raptors, legislative improvements in the protection of raptors and, not least, the resilience of raptors in the face of continual persecution.

The main development has been the organisation of raptor enthusiasts into an effective monitoring and lobbying force. Raptor Study Groups all over Scotland have been successful in monitoring and raising the profile of birds of prey and in assisting both the RSPB's Species Protection Unit and police Wildlife Crime Officers in matters relating to raptor persecution. The network of raptor study groups was founded in 1981 in the northeast of Scotland with the express aims of organizing more effective monitoring of the raptor populations and avoiding duplication of effort and disturbance. By 1985, there were five groups, by 1996, eight, and today there are eleven. This gives good coverage across Scotland and greatly assists the RSPB Species Protection Officers who were instrumental in supporting these initiatives in the early days. Such has been the success of the groups that like-minded fieldworkers in England, Wales and Northern Ireland have followed the Scottish model, now highly regarded worldwide.

*Graham Stewart, Dick Roxburgh, Duncan Cameron and Richard Mearns, part of the early raptor group*

My local group, the South West Scotland Raptor Study Group, was formed in 1983 and the first meeting was held, appropriately enough, in the late Dick Roxburgh's house. Dick was

*Early 1970s pain – it's the peregrine*
*claws you don't see!*

*Ian Hopkins, the roving peregrine*
*warden in southwest Scotland*

an ardent hillwalker in upland Ayrshire and Galloway and in the 1960s had become concerned with and then involved in addressing the predicament of the peregrine, in particular. Slowly, a team began to form round Dick, stimulated by the need to monitor accurately and counteract the extra pressures of eggs and young being stolen by collectors, or destroyed by pigeon fanciers and gamekeepers. I joined the then loose ranks as an 'apprentice' in 1972, inspired by J. A. Baker's book *The Peregrine*. The figures will emphasise the situation at that time: in 1973, we ringed 11 young peregrines and only seven the following year. Twenty years later, over 120 were known to have fledged in the same geographical area.

The fieldwork was stimulating, lessons were quickly learned and experience gained. Memories include being dangled over cliffs on Dick's famous rope, affectionately known as 'the knicker elastic'. It was simply a case of tying it round your waist and down you went. In 1973, the RSPB funded a warden in the southwest with Ian Hopkins from Bute and, later, Richard Mearns filling the role until 1978, supported by the wider and growing group of raptor enthusiasts.

This existing team of fieldworkers formalised into one of the early Raptor Study Groups which, ten years later, would cover southwest Scotland. Luckily, we had at that time some exceptional role models in Donald Watson with his hen harrier work in Galloway, Ian Newton with his sparrowhawk work in Dumfries-shire and Derek Ratcliffe with his near-legendary coverage of peregrine eyries across the region. These men inspired and gave direction to the early group members, many of whom are still active in the field.

Gradually the group expanded, expertise improved and more comprehensive coverage was achieved. By 1991, the group had grown sufficiently to warrant a division into the South Strathclyde Group and the Dumfries and Galloway Group, although there is still dual membership and a lot of interaction between the two. Recognition came too, that year, for Dick Roxburgh, who was presented with the RSPB President's Award for his contribution to raptor work. Sadly, the old warhorse died in 2001.

Nationally, the Raptor Study Groups now consist of around 240 enthusiastic fieldworkers, the majority of whom are volunteers, playing an invaluable role in contributing accurate data on raptor numbers, breeding performance and persecution both on an annual basis and at times of national species surveys. Some of the runs of data now stretch back over decades and are vital in defending the raptors' corner against vociferous opposition and often dubious reports and alleged population statistics. The data also helps the UK to fulfil its international obligation on maintaining the conservation status of raptors.

National conferences have been held since 1991 and the profile of the movement as an independent voice has grown considerably. In 2009 the Scottish Raptor Study Groups hosted the prestigious Raptor Research Foundation annual conference, with 300 raptor experts from 34 countries gathering at the Atholl Palace Hotel in Pitlochry. This was the first time the conference had been held outside the USA.

*Three very influential figures – Dick Roxburgh, Donald Watson and Derek Ratcliffe*

*Part of the Scottish organising team at the Raptor Research Foundation Conference at Pitlochry, 2009, the first time the event had been held outside the USA*

The groups operate under license from Scottish Natural Heritage who also provide some financial assistance to the monitoring process. From the early role of pure monitoring, the groups have been forced into conservation politics and the succession of meetings, email communication, dealing with the media, letter writing and working with other organisations is now a key element in the work, as issues are raised and problem areas exposed. The information collected is now used not just for raptor conservation but extensively in countryside planning matters related to land use. This robust data is vital in combating the often exaggerated and inaccurate claims by the anti-raptor lobby of an 'explosion of raptors'.

The data was originally published annually as the Raptor Report in the Scottish Ornithologist Club's *Scottish Bird News* but now the Scottish Raptor Monitoring Scheme has taken on this role and has also employed a Raptor Monitoring Officer, currently Brian Etheridge, to collate the huge amount of data collected each year. The scheme, chaired by Scottish Natural Heritage, is a partnership between RSPB Scotland, BTO Scotland, SOC, SNH, JNCC, the Scottish Raptor Study Groups and the Rare Breeding Birds Panel. This partnership oversees the monitoring, produced the acclaimed *Raptors: a Field Guide for Surveys and Monitoring* and has initiated framework analyses of the conservation status of the golden eagle, hen harrier and peregrine falcon. In 2009 the scheme was given the Institute of Ecology and Environmental Management Award acknowledging work to the highest standard in ecology in the UK. Roseanna Cunningham MSP, Minister for the Environment in the Scottish Government, said, 'Our birds of prey are part of our unique heritage. Research is vital if we are to help these magnificent creatures thrive and this award shows that Scotland's work is leading the way here and further afield.'

Another major bonus has been the improvement in field techniques and the phenomenal advances in related technologies which have added to the tools at the disposal of raptor workers. There are several excellent texts now available covering raptor monitoring and research: *Raptors: a Field Guide for Surveys and Monitoring* (Hardey *et al.* 2006), *Bird Monitoring Methods* (Gilbert *et al.* 1998), *Bird Census Techniques* (Bibby *et al.* 1992), *Raptor Research and Management Techniques* (Bird and Bildstein 2007) and *Bird Ecology and Conservation* (Sutherland *et al.* 2004).

Computerisation and information technology have meant that records can be collated and presented so much more easily now – memories of playing the osprey conservation game on an Amstrad Integra 2000 now seem very distant. The identification of nesting birds can be checked using microchips called passive integrated transponders, or pit tags, and radio telemetry allows the movement of birds to be mapped accurately. The satellite tracking of individual ospreys and honey buzzards on migration can now be followed on the internet, not only providing superb data but allowing thousands of people to take part virtually in the process. Webcams at nest sites are able to record behaviour and feeding rates and allow the identification and analysis of prey. The most stunning example was illustrated by R.W. Nelson in a presentation at the Raptor Research Foundation Conference in Pitlochry in 2009: video coverage of migratory peregrines from Alaska fighting over territories, occasionally with fatal consequences. Similarly, the images of a peregrine in Derby bringing back a live woodcock on a clear frosty night just before Christmas, having earlier that evening brought in a common snipe, appeared to be the first footage to be shown in public of this species hunting at night (*British Birds* 2010).

Natural Research Ltd., in collaboration with the Scottish Raptor Study Groups, is conducting non-invasive genetic monitoring at Scottish golden eagle nests. DNA extracted from moulted feathers is being used to assess the turnover of adult breeding birds, and their nestlings are being mouth-swabbed so that their DNA can be used to monitor their long-term survival rates. Preliminary results from this research have already led to an intriguing discovery: contrary to the long-held belief that golden eagle pairs are highly territorial, DNA from eagles other than the resident pair has been collected from several nests during the height of the breeding season.

Whatever the technological advances, though, the same basic attributes of patience, attention to detail, hard physical work and absolute commitment, as possessed by hardy pioneers like Seton Gordon and H. B. Macpherson, are still fundamental to fieldwork.

*More sophisticated techniques like DNA testing are helping to break new ground in raptor research*

Among the positive moves in conservation are the reintroduction schemes, instigated to restore populations either lost to Britain by persecution or very restricted in range because of it. The white-tailed sea eagle and the red kite fall into these respective categories but their stories clearly illustrate the differing timescales in their breeding strategies. Naturally, any reintroduction scheme is fraught with problems, not least because of the ethical ladder which first has to be climbed and the stringent criteria which must be laid down and met to ensure that the environment is capable of supporting reintroduced stock.

The choice of release point is critical in giving the birds the best possible start and the first venture – the release in 1959 of three sea eagles released in Glen Etive in Argyll – was a failure. The RSPB chose Fair Isle, a former breeding station, for the next attempt. In 1968, four young sea eagles were hacked back to the wild and although the attempt did not result in breeding success, lessons were learned and techniques developed. By the time the next major release programme was launched on Rum in 1975, the chances of success were much higher. Between 1975 and 1985, 82 young sea eagles were flown in from Norway, with the assistance of the RAF well-documented and maximising publicity. On completing their development, these birds were released into the wild. The fascinating story is recounted in John Love's book *The Return of the Sea Eagle* (1983) and is well worth the read. The establishment of a breeding population has been a slow business but that is hardly a surprise, as eagles in general are not prolific breeders, taking several years to reach maturity and even then producing only small broods, often singles. The first wild chick was not raised until 1985 and a second phase of releasing began in 1993, to enhance the nucleus of birds. In 1995, ten pairs held territory in

Scotland, seven pairs hatched young and five pairs fledged young. In 2010, 46 chicks were successfully hatched by 52 breeding pairs, the highest level in 150 years. There are now over 200 sea eagles in Scotland, representing a huge effort by many dedicated people over the past 30 years. Surely anyone who has seen this magnificent bird in the air, especially above our native coastal cliffs, can only marvel at the spectacle and wish the species well.

*Left: Sea eagles are now becoming established breeders in Scotland and the population is expanding slowly*

*Below left: Bob Swann approaches the wary eaglet*

*Below right: A docile sea eaglet is tagged*

When I was young, my favourite card from all those collected from tea, soap, tobacco and co-operative products was the sea eagle, proudly portrayed on a cliff ledge. Never in my wildest dreams did I envisage that one day I would actually be present at the ringing and wing-tagging of a youngster on a Scottish cliff.

The sea eagle is a classic example of just how time-consuming a reintroduction programme can be and how difficult it is for larger, slow-breeding species to make a comeback. Contrast this with the red kite programme. Confined to a limited range in Wales for most of the last century, the remnant population limped on despite intense positive publicity and protection measures. A reintroduction programme began in southern England and northern Scotland in 1989 and progress has been swift. In 1995, 20 pairs held territory in Scotland, 15 nests were found and ten pairs produced 26 fledged young. Since then, several other schemes have seen birds released in different parts of Britain and Ireland and the breeding population grows annually. Sadly, though, so does the death toll. Vulnerable to poisoning, large numbers of birds, even as many as a third of the birds released in Scotland, have probably been killed in this way, and there are major concerns that the population in north Scotland has failed to increase in recent years as a result.

The impact of poisoning, to which the red kite is especially vulnerable due to its scavenging mode of hunting, is nowhere better illustrated that in the comparison between the progress of the releases of red kites in the Chilterns and northern Scotland. There is a huge difference in the progress of the two populations. By 2006, the north Scotland population had reached 41 pairs compared with more than 300 in the Chilterns, despite the fact that the two programmes had started at roughly the same time. Illegal killing was responsible for 55% of north Scotland's red kites recovered dead, where a cause of death could be established. The vast majority of those killed were victims of carrion bait laced with poison (Smart *et al.* 2010), surely an unacceptable state of affairs in this day and age.

*Red kite population expansion*

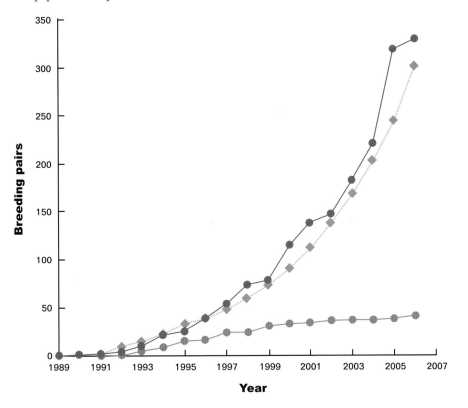

Orange circles/solid orange line: observed population trajectory of red kite for north Scotland

Red circles/solid red line: trajectory for red kites in the Chilterns

Green diamonds/dashed green line: models the north Scotland population's trajectory using survival rates adjusted assuming the removal of illegal killing

I would certainly hope to see red kites breeding in Ayrshire soon and maybe, on a longer timescale, sea eagles back in their old haunts on Ailsa Craig and Arran off the Ayrshire coast.

What has been particularly gratifying is that Scottish birds have been used to assist in the reintroduction of both golden eagles and ospreys to the Republic of Ireland and England respectively. Roy Dennis' work with the relevant government bodies and Anglian Water paved the way for the translocation of young osprey chicks to Rutland Water, where they were cared for and eventually released into the wild. As a result, ospreys now breed in the English Midlands and youngsters from there have begun breeding in Wales.

*Right: Roy Dennis, a prime mover in the reintroduction project*

*Below left: Kevin Lawler and Winnie Mackinnon with Red L*

*Below right: Red L secured and ready to transport*

The Irish Golden Eagle Reintroduction Project, under the direction of the enthusiastic Lorcan O'Toole, has spearheaded the return of the golden eagle to Ireland. Chicks of 5–6 weeks old were transported from nests in Scotland to Glenveagh National Park in County Donegal and released once they were ready to fly. Single birds were taken from the nests of known productive pairs which had twins. The first breeding took place in 2005.

Scottish Raptor Study Groups were involved in collecting the chicks from nests and I was lucky enough to assist on a couple of occasions. This is my diary extract from 28 June 2008:

> Up early and prepared for what was expected to be a very exciting day. Outside the bothy, while waiting to be picked up, a very strident song caught my attention. Unbelievably, a common rosefinch male was in full voice high in the tree adjacent to the building. Just to confirm the identification it flew down and fed among the weed seeds by the roadside – a good omen for the day.
>
> Off in a crowded Land Rover with Kevin Lawler, the climber, to the nearest parking spot then off over the rough terrain. My job: carrying the box. Disappointingly, the 500-foot cliffs were shrouded in mist and despite telescope work by Kevin and Martin, it was unclear if there were two eaglets in the eyrie. I certainly could see one through my binoculars but as soon as it lay down, I could see very little. The huge stick nest was tiny to the naked eye, perched as it was in a cutting well down the intimidating cliffs which descended precipitously to the sea below.
>
> The decision was made to go ahead so we proceeded to the top of the cliff to the point which had been identified as being directly above the nest. The mist slipped in and out as the belay was set up and Kevin joined two ropes to cover his 250-foot descent. He disappeared over the cliff edge and for the next hour and a half we waited anxiously, although as time passed we realized that a positive outcome was on the cards. Of the adult eagles there was no sign.
>
> Thankfully the white helmet appeared over the cliff top and an exhausted Kevin hauled himself up. He had had trouble with the join in the rope and was quite dehydrated but the bird was in the haversack. Once the ropes were hauled up and the kit sorted, the seven-week-old female was transferred – with not a little difficulty – into the carrying box. She was in excellent feather condition, weighed a ton and was far from docile. There was little down on her plumage. The weight of the bird was such that we had to take turns carrying it back but two sightings of kestrels hovering kept us going!
>
> Back at the bothy we enjoyed a welcome beer as the bird left to begin its journey to Donegal.

Red L, as she was called, was last seen on 20 February the following year and although no contact has been made since, it is hoped she will survive her first few years wandering. Another female, Green H, was collected in 2004, and a male, White 4, in 2006, one of only four birds collected that year. This male had to be returned to captivity after ten days as he had been found in a weak condition. He was later released once he had picked up again. He had been much smaller than his female sibling so he might not have survived at all had he remained in the nest

Having benefited from other countries' generosity with the red kite and sea eagle reintroductions, it is fitting that we have been able to assist others in their attempts to diversify their raptor populations. With widespread and worrying declines of red kites on the Continent, who knows what the future will hold? Ireland, too, is suffering from the scourge of poisoning and the loss of released birds is causing concern.

*Above: Red L flying free in Ireland as part of the reintroduction scheme*

*Right: Justin Grant about to descend the cliff to collect the golden eagle chick*

*Below right: The author with Green H, a young female*

*Below left: Young male, White 4, ringed and ready to go*

*Opposite page: Irish and Scottish members of the Irish Golden Eagle Reintroduction scheme*

Not all the positive changes have been brought about deliberately by man: some species have taken advantage of changing conditions. These 'cultural' changes have helped some raptors to spread and others to improve their chances of breeding success. The sparrowhawk, for example, has moved into cities where it is quite at home nesting in wooded cemeteries, parks and gardens. More spectacular has been the establishment of peregrine territories in many busy cities where high buildings act as surrogate cliffs and there is no lack of urban bird prey. Ospreys, too, are now nesting on the relative safety of electricity pylons.

Even more astonishing is the totally unexpected phenomenon of a ground-nesting species like the hen harrier beginning to nest in trees. It could only happen in Northern Ireland! In 1991, a pair attempted to breed in a sitka spruce plantation, in a tree which had lost its leader and where the topmost branches had formed a suitable nesting platform. Since then, Don Scott (Scott 2008) has monitored this trend as several pairs used deformed spruce tops as nest sites. The breeding attempts have not been without their problems, with instances of eggs and young falling through insubstantial structures. The older youngsters are naturally adventurous and in ground nests are often found off the nest and in the surrounding heather – not a behavioral trait to have twenty feet up a sitka!

Although the tree-nesting may only be a quirk in one small area of its range, utilising a range of woodland habitats for ground-nesting may turn out to be much more advantageous. In western Scotland a significant proportion of hen harriers are now breeding in woodland habitats, including mature and second-rotation conifer plantations, newly-planted native woodland and regenerating woodland and scrub (Haworth and Fielding 2009). These woodland habitats offer harriers a nesting environment where human persecution is less likely. Second-rotation planting also offers much more cover and could also reduce predation, although there is a question mark over densities and accessibility of prey. These are early days but if it becomes a widespread trend then it can only be positive for this hard-pressed bird of prey.

All these fascinating stories have been instrumental in stimulating in the past quarter century a huge interest in wildlife conservation in general and in raptors in particular. Attitudes have changed and the general public is much more aware and supportive of causes, thanks in no small measure to the volume and quality of natural history material on television and in print. The publicity given to court cases involving the persecution of birds of prey does stir up emotions, not only against the perpetrators but also against those who turn a blind eye. The killing of a golden eagle in the Scottish Borders in 2007 caused a furore not just among the bird fraternity but among the public in general. The poisoning of Alma, the young golden eagle which had been satellite tagged by Roy Dennis in July 2009, generated considerable national and international publicity. Thousands of people had followed with great interest the bird's progress on the Highland Foundation for Wildlife website. The young honey buzzard from the Highlands which took a wrong turn and ended up hundreds of miles out in the Atlantic made the national news and created headlines in newspapers. The sudden deterioration in health of Lady, the veteran osprey female at her nest at the Loch of the Lowes, was followed by a worldwide audience of enthusiasts and, as the drama unfolded, was eagerly covered by television and newspapers.

Raptors nesting in odd places like cranes, aircraft and window boxes in flats regularly feature in newspapers. Nest box schemes are promoted in many areas of the country for kestrels and barn owls, and working with schools and young people is now standard in any conservation organisation's core activities. The importance of this cannot be overstated and the impact of this support is huge and will continue to grow.

For many people, the sight of a kestrel hovering, a buzzard soaring, a hen harrier sky-dancing above heather moorland or, best of all, the glimpse of the blue riband of raptors, the magnificent golden eagle, is an enormous pleasure. Anyone who ignores this powerful lobby is misguided. The organisation which comes in for most vitriol from the game-rearing fraternity and the pigeon fanciers is the RSPB, yet the support they have for their work is phenomenal – a powerful mandate from over one million members. A look at the membership size of the main political parties or the anti-raptor groups will put this into its true perspective.

Closely allied to this awareness is the economic picture in the countryside, which has changed dramatically. One of the main arguments put forward by the anti-raptor lobby is that the bird of prey 'explosion' is negatively affecting quarry species on sporting estates and that the knock-on effect will be unemployment in the countryside. Apart from there being very little evidence that this would be the case in many areas, this argument also completely ignores that fact that the number of people directly involved with sporting estates has been dwindling for a long time. Around 25,000 gamekeepers were employed at the beginning of the century, a figure which has decreased to 2,000 and the downward spiral will probably continue. The days of the huge country estates employing large numbers of staff are gone. That is not to say that these jobs are not important, but when set against the huge numbers of people and the vast spend involved in wildlife-watching, a degree of perspective dawns.

An increasing number of people are employed in the conservation field in Scotland, in nature reserves, national parks, country parks, research work or wildlife outlets. Look at the economic benefits to Speyside of initiatives such as Operation Osprey at Boat of Garten, which attracts thousands of visitors annually to the area with all the attendant spin-offs. Scotland's five osprey-watching sites attracted approximately 125,000 visitors in 2005 and they spent an estimated £2.19 million in the areas around the sites. On 9 August 2002 the Loch Garten Osprey Centre welcomed its two millionth visitor.

On the Isle of Mull, which attracts 350,000 visitors every year, the total annual spend by visitors is £38 million. The visitor spend attracted by sea eagles is estimated to be £1.4–£1.6 million (Dickie *et al.* 2006). In Dumfries and Galloway the Kite trail is estimated to have generated £21 million for the local economy since 2003.

The practice of using remote cameras at raptor nest sites and relaying the daily soap opera to visitor centres has also been successfully pioneered with the red kite, goshawk, hen harrier, peregrine, kestrel and white-tailed sea eagle. What potential, what drawing power! How often does the golden eagle or buzzard feature on national and local tourist material?

Grouse shooting is very important in Scotland, generating £17 million per annum, but recent Visit Scotland data identifies £212 million income from walking trips in the countryside and a further £74 million from wildlife and nature-watching holidays, totals which I am sure will continue to grow and add to the economy of the Scottish countryside. I hope the same will be true of the shooting interest, but the continual bad press and bad practice linked to raptor persecution does no one any favours.

The kite trail in Galloway, the feeding station in Stirlingshire and kite viewing at the Black Isle; the osprey centres at Boat of Garten, Loch of the Lowes, the Tweed Valley and Wigtown; the eagle experience on the Isle of Mull; peregrine-watching at Queen Elizabeth Forest Park and the Falls of Clyde; the hen harrier at Clyde Muirshiel Regional Park and Forsinard in the Highlands. All these and many smaller initiatives are examples in Scotland of what is happening across the UK and are important integral parts of local economies. Raptors are now a precious economic commodity in some rural communities and are putting money in wage packets. At the same time, let us lay the ghost of the urban vs rural debate. The rural economy could not survive without the influx of urban visitors for recreational pursuits, injecting much-needed revenue into bed and breakfasts, holiday lets, crofts, transport and much more.

*The kite trail in Galloway – a vital spin-off in the local economy*

Protective legislation has been one of the main strands in the battle to restore the raptor populations to levels that match the carrying capacity of the diverse habitats in Britain. Most raptors have been fully protected in law since 1954, the exception being the sparrowhawk, which only received full protection in 1961 after the pesticide-induced crash. This was reinforced when, under the Wildlife and Countryside Act (1981), all birds of prey and owls, their nests, eggs and young became fully protected at all times. Special protection is offered to all birds categorised as Schedule 1, namely the golden eagle, goshawk, all species of harrier, hobby, honey buzzard, merlin, osprey, peregrine and white-tailed eagle.

Stronger laws to protect Scottish wildlife came into force following the establishment of the Scottish Parliament but are applicable only to Scotland. The Nature Conservation (Scotland) Act 2004 and the Criminal Justice (Scotland) Act 2003 are now key pieces of legislation. The latter allows courts to jail wildlife crime offenders for up to six months as well as impose fines of up to £5,000 per offence, reflecting the public's abhorrence of such crimes. Police forces have enhanced powers, including provisions for arrest and obtaining warrants for a broader range of offences.

Of the 15 raptor species breeding in Britain, 11 are red data birds and nine are of conservation concern on an international scale. Britain holds 13%–14% of the European populations of peregrines, sparrowhawks and kestrels and 7% of golden eagles. This European dimension is also enshrined in legislation as the European Community Directive on the Conservation of Wild Birds (79/409) which requires member states to take special conservation measures for Annex One species including golden eagle, hen harrier, peregrine falcon, white-tailed sea eagle, red kite, osprey and merlin. So far so good: the foundation stones are in place.

Sadly, legislation has only proved successful up to a point and there are still hurdles to negotiate. Positive steps forward, such as the establishment of a network of Wildlife Crime Officers, have been hampered by the fact that wildlife crime does not come high on the agenda of many police forces or even, sometimes, of the judiciary itself. Despite the best efforts of dedicated officers, the Investigations Section of RSPB Scotland and raptor workers, wildlife crime continues to be a blight on the Scottish countryside. It is extremely frustrating that even when convictions have been secured, the sentencing has often not been strong enough to act as a real deterrent. Custodial sentences are few and far between, and none have been imposed in Scotland so far. Killing raptors tarnishes the gamekeeping profession and if it does not stop, tighter regulation must come, possibly involving the licensing of sporting estates and vicarious liability where employers and owners will be held responsible for raptors killed on their ground. This is not an attack on responsible landowners and managers, of which there are many, but on the estates where persecution has been shown to be a significant and consistent problem. The people who carry out the persecution do their profession and Scotland's natural heritage a great disservice.

In May 2010 a letter was sent to Roseanna Cunningham, the Environment Minister, from 200 Scottish landowners demanding action to end the illegal poisoning of raptors. They not only denounced the activity but also called for the full weight of the law to be brought to bear on anyone found guilty of this criminal activity. While welcoming the sentiment, I would say that words are easy and that progress will only be made if the words are firmly translated down the line to the perpetrators, or to those landlords who condone poisoning or turn a blind eye to it. The track record is not encouraging.

*Sadly our national icon continues to be persecuted on sporting estates, a blight on Scotland's heritage*

The damning facts are to be seen in figures published, for example, in the RSPB's persecution reports on offences against raptors. Year after year these make dismal reading. Other publications which add to the evidence of persecution are *Counting the Cost – the Continuing Persecution of Birds of Prey in Scotland*, published by the Scottish Office in 1998, and *The Illegal Persecution of Raptors in Scotland*, also from the Scottish Office in the same year. *Birds of Prey in the UK: Back from the Brink*, published by a consortium of non-government bodies, revised in 1999, gives a clear account of a situation that continues today. The recent map of bird poisonings in Scotland (PAW Scotland 2009), the notorious 'map of shame', backed by the Scottish Government, shows the hotspots, locating 88 incidents over the past five years. As recently as May 2010, three golden eagles were found dead from poisoning, bringing the tally to 14 killed illegally in the last ten years. Many fieldworkers feel that this is only the tip of the iceberg, as much criminal activity takes place in remote areas where it is extremely difficult to obtain evidence.

Thankfully, there has been a growing political will to address this problem. It's a damming indictment of the way we treat this vital part of Scotland's natural heritage, which sadly puts us on a par with Malta, Cyprus and Italy where the shooting of raptors is also still a major environmental problem. The late Donald Dewar, First Minister in the Scottish Executive, was to the fore on this issue, labeling the illegal killing of raptors 'a national disgrace'. This has been followed by similar supportive quotes from ministers and members of the Scottish Parliament.

Environment Minister Michael Russell MSP said at the launch of the RSPB Bird of Prey campaign in 2008:

'Birds of prey are among Scotland's finest national assets and I welcome any action to ensure that remains the case. Recent reports of the persecution of raptors have been very disturbing and the pledge I am signing today will be an important means of protecting these wonderful species.'

Roseanna Cunningham MSP and currently Environment Minister declared at the Wildlife Crime debate of 2007:

'Arguments are made about the threat that sparrowhawks pose to racing pigeons or that hen harriers pose to grouse chicks, but the most dangerous predator of all is the two-legged wingless poisoner, which needs to become a good deal rarer'.

The late Magnus Magnusson, when SNH Chairman, threw down the gauntlet at the feet of those who manage the countryside when he launched the Wildlife Liaison Officer Conference at Tulliallan in February 1999:

'Can you show society that you can manage the land well without breaking the law? Can you deliver a moratorium on the illegal persecution of birds of prey? Can you prove to us that golden eagles, peregrines and hen harriers will not be tampered with on your estate? So here is my specific plea I want to see the year 2000 remembered as the 'Persecution-Free Year'. Surely we can stamp out wildlife crime in Scotland?'

However, despite ministerial condemnation, despite the work of Wildlife Crime Officers, the RSPB Investigations Section, the SSPCA and raptor workers, birds of prey are still persecuted on some sporting estates, particularly on driven grouse moors. In some circles, there is a culture of denial that the level of persecution which is regularly exposed even exists, and a feeling that the current laws are bad laws. Make no mistake: there is a very powerful lobby, linked to the game management business, well-funded and politically strong, whose idea of balance in the countryside equates with raptor control and who are working tirelessly to change the laws – back to those of Victorian times. The cry is for a quota system and translocation, which would be virtually impossible to monitor even if deemed an acceptable practice. It would be a licence to kill by another name and I cannot see landowners queuing up to take young harriers onto their ground!

There are, thankfully, more enlightened people who are working towards solutions. Co-operative initiatives such as the diversionary feeding experiments at the Langholm Demonstration Project, Operation Countrywatch in Perthshire, Falcon 2000 in northeast Scotland, the Moorland Forum, Special Protection Areas for hen harriers and golden eagles and the Partnership Against Wildlife Crime all contribute towards addressing these issues.

The table opposite shows clearly that the position is considerably healthier than in 1972, when I began my work with kestrels, and accurately reflects the fact that raptor populations are in better shape that at any time in the last hundred years. We still have a long way to go: the school report might read, 'Progress, but still much room for improvement'. Persecution must come to an absolute stop if any meaningful decisions are to be made involving the manipulation of raptor populations by whatever technique. We need to build up a level of trust which does not exist at present and, more importantly, allow some raptor populations to begin to reach natural and sustainable levels. We need to see greater accountability on the part of landowners and managers, more Wildlife Crime Officers, intelligence-led policing, a more serious approach to wildlife crime on the part of the police and judiciary and the adoption of best practice

*UK Raptor Population Levels   1972–2006*

|  | Newton 1972 | Newton 1993–4 | Baker et al 2006 |
|---|---|---|---|
| Kestrel | 60,000 | 60,000 | 35,400 |
| Sparrowhawk | 15–20,000 | 30,000 | 38,600 |
| Buzzard | 8–10,000 | 20,000 | 44,000 |
| Merlin | 600–800 | 1,300 | 1,300 |
| Peregrine | 378 | 1,200 | 1,167 |
| Goshawk | 10–20 | 300 | 400 |
| Remainder | 1,064 | 1,440 | 3,981 |
| **Total** | **92,269** | **114,240** | **124,848** |
| **Kestrel %** | **65** | **52** | **28** |

with non-lethal methods and habitat management. Public awareness is at an all-time high, the much- maligned RSPB has a voice backed by over a million members and Government condemnation of persecution is strong. It would be an achievement if the momentum could be maintained and this period be remembered as a time when raptors flourished, a sign of good health in our environment. The saddest thing is that the perpetrators of illegal persecution – the so-called stewards of the countryside – are unable to appreciate those icons of the Scottish wildlife heritage: the uplifting sight of a golden eagle soaring over a glen or the stunning sky dancing hen harrier gracing a heather moor.

# 8

## *Readjustment*

So how has the kestrel fared? The end of the 20th century and the beginning of the 21st saw a change in the status of the kestrel in Britain which could never have been anticipated in the early 1970s. It would have been hard to believe that within a few decades, the kestrel would be relegated to third in the list of our mot common raptors, behind the buzzard and the sparrowhawk, when at one time the number of breeding pairs exceeded the combined total of all other raptor species. In many ways it is a reflection of the massive changes that have taken place in the raptor landscape of Britain.

As usual, the picture is complex and in order to understand the current state of affairs it is worth looking for pointers in the history of the kestrel over the last century. Compared with more spectacular raptors such as the osprey, peregrine and golden eagle, the kestrel has never been a flagship species and has had relatively few advocates, with a few notable exceptions such as the late Eddie Balfour on Orkney, Andy Village (*The Kestrel* 1990), Mike Shrubb (*The Kestrel*, 1993) and myself (*Seasons with the Kestrel*, 1992). What has always surprised me is that so few people have seen the advantages of monitoring and studying kestrels, as they take readily to nest box schemes and because, quite simply, there are more of them than there are of most species and so can provide quantitative data. Maybe it is that very abundance which explains the dearth of fieldwork, with people putting more effort into species of conservation concern, particularly in the wake of the disastrous pesticide period. In the USA and Holland, by comparison, the American and common kestrel respectively have massive coverage and nest box schemes are utilised to great effect.

The kestrel did not escape the late-19th century persecution of birds of prey in the name of game rearing and there were serious declines in parts of Britain. Although opportunist kestrels no doubt visited rearing pens and took game birds chicks in the wild, their impact on game rearing must have been fairly negligible. It was simply a crime to have a hooked beak and talons, and they therefore appeared regularly on gamekeepers' gibbets, on bounty lists and vermin tallies. The kestrel may have been tolerated by some keepers due to its small mammal diet but as Charles St. John commented in 1919, that would have been the exception rather than the rule:

*Nest boxes can aid*
*monitoring*

'I never shoot at, or disturb a kestrel. It is impossible however to persuade a gamekeeper that any bird called a hawk can be harmless; much less can one persuade so opinionated and conceited a personage (as most keepers are) that a hawk can be useful; therefore the poor kestrel generally occupies a prominent place among the rows of bipeds and quadrupeds nailed on the kennel or wherever else those trophies of his skill are exhibited.'

Bob MacMillan on the Isle of Skye has done some recent research into estate game books and the number of kestrels killed is surprisingly high. On the Borline Estate on Skye between 1895 and 1898, 61 kestrels were killed, along with a further 28 between 1909 and 1918. Similarly, 63 kestrels were killed on Glen Shieldaig between 1874 and 1892, while 29 were on the vermin list for Erchless Estate, Beauly between 1873 and 1877. Individual records on the Borline Estate six, five and four kestrels killed on days in the later part of the breeding seasons, indicating in all probability that the keeper was specifically targeting broods. The toll was indeed high and almost certainly worse than these figures suggest because the kestrel probably figured as a large proportion of those recorded in a general category, 'hawks'.

In the early years of the 20th century the position improved slightly as persecution decreased, especially during the two world wars when many gamekeepers were serving in the armed forces. From the 1930s onwards the kestrel began to colonise urban areas, particularly after 1945, but this move was unfortunately followed by a marked decline in the late 1950s and early 1960s when raptor populations were decimated by pesticide poisoning caused by the agricultural practice of using organochlorine chemicals as seed dressing. Kestrels were by no means immune to the detrimental side effects of pesticides such as DDT and Dieldrin which accumulated through feeding on seed-eating small mammals and birds, the mainstay of their diet.

By the time I became involved with the kestrel in early 1972, these pesticides had been withdrawn from use and the kestrel had once more staged a recovery. In the 1968–1972 *Atlas of Breeding Birds in Britain and Ireland* (Sharrock 1976) the kestrel was put at the top end of the 10,000 to 100,000 pairs bracket. This was the first real attempt at estimating population

*Despite its feeding habits, no exception was made for kestrels in the persecution frenzy*

170

*The kestrel is far from immune from pesticide poisoning*

*Five strapping youngsters, feisty to handle*

size and was based upon the coverage of ten-kilometre squares by an impressive team of 10,000 birdwatchers. The kestrel was recorded in 3,546 squares, 92% of the total, and possible breeding was recorded in 13%, probable breeding in 13% and confirmed breeding in 75%. The general conclusion was that the kestrel was the most widespread and numerous raptor in Britain although it may have been outnumbered by the sparrowhawk in some locations.

The main areas of absence were identified as Shetland, where the kestrel had last nested in 1905, and much of the Outer Hebrides. Low density in the western Highlands was seen to be related to high precipitation which adversely affects the kestrel's hunting technique and the above-ground activity of its prey.

Decreases had been detected in the numbers of kestrels in the eastern English counties from the mid-1950s onwards, the exceptions being pockets of non-agricultural land within these areas such as the Broads and Breckland in East Anglia. There was also a co-incidental decline in parts of Ireland. A lack of breeding records in much of the Fen country of eastern England suggested that the kestrel was scarce there.

The calculation was made, taking all Common Bird Censuses into consideration, that there was an average of 75 pairs of kestrels per ten-kilometre square in 1972: 'Even if the density over the whole of Britain and Ireland was about half of this figure, the total would be at or above the upper limit of Parslaw's 10,000 to 100,000 pairs.'

At this time the kestrel was not only common but was enjoying a good press due to novel choices of nest sites in urban settings, which fueled local interest. Hunting motorway verges, being the emblem of the junior branch of the RSPB and featuring prominently on a lager can maintained its high profile.

One setback of note was the response to Ken Loach's superb film *Kes*, inspired by Barry Hines' fine social portrait *A Kestrel for a Knave*. The downside of seeing a boy gaining self-esteem from taking and training a kestrel from the wild was that it encouraged hundreds of children to try their hand at it. This led to the deaths of many young birds when the initial enthusiasm and romance gave way to the reality of acquiring food and spending long hours in training. Kestrels in small, unsuitable cages and boxes feature in my memories of the 1970s, as birds were dumped on ornithologists' doorsteps or simply abandoned. Nest failures were regularly attributed to the theft of young birds, whereas now it hardly exists as a problem except in isolated cases. I would like to think that this is the result of good public relations and environmental education but I suspect that youngsters have simply become more sedentary in their habits and spend their time staring at monitors rather than exploring the countryside near their homes. We have a generation of highly environmentally-aware children but few practical naturalists.

*Youngster in very poor condition after being abandoned by children*

Ian Newton, in his review of the raptors in Britain in 1984, stated that only one species, the kestrel, could be considered as being close to the level that the available habitat could support. Some changes, however, became apparent in the results for the *New Atlas of Breeding Birds in Britain and Ireland* of 1988–1991 (Gibbons *et al.* 1993). The abundance maps suggested that the previously reported scarcity of kestrels in northwest Scotland extended to Ireland, southeast Wales and parts of southwest England and that the scarcity in the Outer Hebrides and Shetland had not changed since the first *Atlas* assessment. In comparison, what had changed markedly was that the main strongholds now included parts of southeast Britain, particularly East Anglia, which 20 years previously had been recorded as poorly occupied. This suggested an apparent decline in the west and recovery in the southeast of Britain.

Where breeding in Britain had been measured accurately, it varied from about 36 pairs per 100 km² in good vole years in grassland to ten pairs per 100 km² in intensive arable farmland. Andy Village calculated that the mean density for the whole of Britain was probably nearer 20 pairs per 100 km² and that if this was applied to the 2,481 occupied ten-kilometre squares, the range of the British population was in the 25,000 to 89,000 pairs bracket, likely averaging at around 50,000 pairs (Village 1986, Gibbons *et al.* 1993).

Valerie Thom reported in her book *Birds in Scotland* (1986) that the BTO's Common Bird Census results indicated that the kestrel population in Scotland was fairly stable. Ian Newton's analysis of the raptor population levels in Britain in 1994 put the kestrel at around 60,000 pairs, stable and almost at capacity level (Newton 1994). It is interesting to note that this total was more than the combined total of all the rest: sparrowhawk were stable at 30,000, buzzard were at 20,000 and increasing, merlin at 1,300 and increasing, peregrine at 1,200 and increasing, with all the others – hen harrier, golden eagle, goshawk, marsh harrier, red kite, osprey and white-tailed eagle – individually under 1,000.

Due to the declines noted in the *Atlas* work, and because of its unfavourable conservation status in Europe, the kestrel was put on the amber list in the Birds of Conservation Concern in the UK, Channel Islands and the Isle of Man published in 1996. This amber status reflected medium conservation concern, the criterion being a 25% to 49% decline in the UK breeding population or range over the previous 25 years.

As the century came to a close the general consensus was pretty unanimous: that the kestrel population in Britain was in partial decline. Commentators such as the late Chris Mead (2000) and data from the British Trust for Ornithology's Common Bird Census and Breeding Bird Survey confirmed the amber status, with declines in the order of 30% in the UK between 1994 and 2002, with England down 23% and Scotland down 42% Within England, the greatest declines had occurred in the southwest, down 51%, and in eastern regions, down 48%. In *The State of the Nation's Birds*, Mead wrote that the kestrel's status was a serious cause for concern.

Although the decline in kestrel numbers was described as moderate, a marked change in status was obviously taking place. The population breakdown in 2000 was estimated at 35,000 pairs of kestrels in England, 11,000 in Scotland, 3,500 in Wales, 1,500 in Northern Ireland and 150 in the Isle of Man (Noble *et al.* 2001). Unpublished BTO figures in 2004 further revised this to a minimum of 36,800 pairs in the UK.

The decline indicators keep coming. The kestrel has now joined the BTO nest record scheme concern list as brood sizes have reduced significantly since the early 1990s, suggesting that more pairs are now rearing three chicks instead of four or five (Leach *et al.* 2006). Furthermore, the BTO's *Breeding Birds in the Wider Countryside* status analysis (Baillie *et al.* 2001) reports that the kestrel population has declined by more than a quarter, especially in lowland England and Wales. Although gauging the kestrel population size is not an exact science, the message is clear. The current estimated population totals are given below.

The most recent BTO Breeding Bird Survey results for 2009 showed that the kestrel decline in Scotland was much greater than in the rest of the UK. The kestrel declined by 54% between 1995 and 2008 with a 64% decline between 2008 and 2009. In the corresponding periods in a UK context the declines were 20% and 36% respectively. This is backed up by the preliminary results for the kestrel from the 2007–2011 *Bird Atlas* which suggest a range contraction in the west, notably in Ireland, southwest England, Wales and northern Scotland. However, coverage is at present incomplete in the west of Britain and Ireland so it is too early to draw too many assumptions from this data about changes in range. Common Bird Survey results from Ireland show a worrying 6.89% decline (Coombes *et al.* 2009) and the Wales Raptor Study Group is 'witnessing a rapid decline in the kestrel as a breeding bird in Wales'.

## Current Kestrel Status

|  | Pairs | Source |
|---|---|---|
| United Kingdom | 35,600 | BTO |
| England and Wales | 26,400 | BTO |
| Scotland | 7,700 | BS3 |
| Northern Ireland | 1,500 | BTO |
| Ireland | 10,000 | Irish RSG |
| Isle of Man | 121–123 | Manx Bird Atlas* |

UK Conservation Status amber – 25-49% population decline. Medium conservation concern

BTO Nest Record Scheme – concern list (* Sharpe, 2007)

European Conservation Status – category SPEC 3 – unfavourable status in Europe 300,000 – 440,000 pairs

Even given the small sample size compared with England and Wales, the Scottish situation merits serious attention. Analysis is notoriously difficult due to the previously-mentioned lack of coverage but a close examination of available data in Scotland reveals a fascinatingly mixed bag, from strong populations in the southwest to scattered low densities in the northwest Highlands.

Scotland supports around 21% of the UK population at 7,765 breeding pairs (Forrester *et al.* 2007). Up until the last decade of the 20th century there was little quantative data to go on although the bird was known to be widespread. The exceptions were Orkney, some areas of Highland, Ayrshire and Eskdalemuir, where a few individuals had concentrated on the kestrel over a reasonable timescale. However, the evolution of the Scottish Raptor Study Groups along with local bird atlas work have raised the level of coverage, resulting in slightly better annual data.

Starting with the Northern Isles, the kestrel is a scarce passage migrant in Shetland and although it is recorded in all months, the peaks are in May and in August–October. Dymond (1991) noted that kestrels may be present on Fair Isle from mid-August to mid-October and during one notable influx in early September 1998 there was a peak of 26 birds. Birds were recorded breeding in 19th century Shetland with most nest sites on sea cliffs, but only two breeding attempts were given credibility during the 20th century. One pair nested in 1905 and another in 1992, using an old raven's nest in a quarry and fledging at least three young. Changes in agricultural practices in Shetland may have resulted in limited prey being available (Pennington *et al.* 2004).

In Orkney the kestrel has seen a downward trend and the 'moosie haak' has gone from being reasonably common in the mid-20th century to being an uncommon resident breeder and uncommon passage visitor today. Between 1972 and 1974 an estimated 63–73 pairs bred annually but by 1997 only a third of that total were breeding. The main reason for the decline is given as habitat change, particularly the loss of moorland and other semi-natural ground which has affected the principal prey item, the Orkney vole (*Microtus arvalis*).

Rough grassland is a critical habitat for Orkney hen harriers. Sheep densities more than doubled between 1975 and 1997 with a corresponding decline in the population densities of both the harrier and the kestrel. Agricultural records indicate that rough grassland was lost to intensive pasture and that overgrazing dramatically reduced the availability of prey such as the Orkney vole. The well-studied harrier population has recovered in the past decade, coinciding with a huge decrease in sheep numbers (Amar *et al.* 2008). The kestrel population declined in parallel with the hen harrier but Eric Meek reports that no noticeable recovery has been noticed with the kestrel. The kestrel population tends to fluctuate and is under-recorded so other factors may be at work.

The loss of corn and haystacks, a haven for small mammals and passerines, was a major factor in diminishing the potential prey available (Booth 2000). There has also been a corresponding reduction in ground-nesting, a phenomenon which was first noticed in 1945 (Balfour 1955) and had become widespread by the 1950s with at least 19 nesting territories being used. The lack of mammalian predators is a key factor as ground-nesting of kestrels on mainland Scotland is a rare occurrence. By 2007, however, only three ground sites were recorded as being used. Substantial efforts are being made by the RSPB to improve some areas of heather moorland in Orkney, which have not been burnt for 30 years, using an imported mulching machine. By diversifying the age range of the heather, the improvement of habitat for breeding hen harriers will be beneficial to the kestrel as well.

By contrast there has been an increase in breeding kestrel pairs in recent years in the Outer Hebrides. The overall total for the islands is in the range of 35–40 pairs. In Lewis and Harris, where voles are absent, there was very little information prior to the late 1990s when a breeding site was found on South Harris. Since then, breeding has been proved on at least three sites on Lewis and possible breeding at five or six other sites. The Lewis and Harris population is currently estimated at 15–25 pairs. There are no records for Barra.

The breeding population on the Uists and Benbecula is 20–25 pairs and, with broods of five and six being recorded, the indications are that the population is quite healthy. Birds are nesting in a range of sites, favouring holes in small crags and overhangs of heather. John Love recorded one adventurous kestrel pair living dangerously by nesting in an alternative sea eagle nest in 2008. There are ground-nesters and merlins may have been replaced in a couple of sites. To complete the Outer Hebrides picture, kestrels occur as migrants and winter visitors as well.

One of my abiding memories of South Uist was of watching a family of merlins on a beautiful sunny morning, The four young were long out of the nest, confident but still being fed by the adults. Each bird perched on a boulder on the glen floor while we watched from a heathery ridge halfway up the hillside. Keith, my son, was particularly agitated by flies buzzing around him and it was only when we got up to leave, and he fell forward, that we realized that he had been lying above the actual nest site, now festering with the debris of a full breeding season. Merlin buffs will appreciate just how lucky that find was, as it can take a huge effort to locate the bird's nest in heather banks.

The area monitored by the Highland Raptor Study Group has seen a steady decline in kestrel breeding attempts since 1990. In one study area the number of pairs fell from 44 to 15. This work has been carried out primarily by Mike Canham who, like me, operates a nest box scheme. Productivity is still high despite the decline: the mean clutch size in 2002 was 5.6 and the brood size 5.3 (Canham 2003). Brian Etheridge, the Raptor Monitoring Officer for Scotland, reckons that the kestrel is now the rarest raptor in most of the Highlands.

Similarly there is a clear decrease in the number of occupied Breeding Bird Survey squares in the northeast of Scotland although the bird is still widespread in the region, probably with around 1000 pairs (Francis and Cook 2011). A ground-nesting record in Donside in 2000 was a rare mainland occurrence. Kestrels are often recorded along the coastline from August to November and these are probably migrants from Scandinavia.

Further south the kestrel is classified as an uncommon breeding resident and scarce passage migrant in the Fife Ornithological Atlas and is widespread in suitable habitat across most of the Kingdom (Elkins 2003). The population, based upon a density of 0.8 pairs per tetrad, is likely to be around 120 pairs in a good vole year dropping to half that number in a lean year. The over-wintering population is unlikely to exceeded 500 birds. Data from the Isle of May indicates that Fife kestrels are joined by small numbers of migrants from Scandinavia with peak passage in September and October. One notable record was of 31 kestrels on one day in mid-September 1969, following a period of strong easterly winds.

A 70% decrease from 31 pairs in 1987–1988 to nine pairs in 1989–1990 in Perth and Kinross accelerated, with Scottish Bird Reports noting only six occupied sites in 2000.

In the southeast of Scotland, analysis of data has shown a general decrease in kestrels recorded from west to east, the bird being more sparsely distributed in parts of East Lothian and the Merse, due probably to large-scale grain cultivation. A look at habitat preferences shows a clear affinity between the kestrel and unimproved land. (Murray *et al.* 1998). Above 500 metres, there is a considerable reduction in the number of breeding pairs. The population estimate of around 1,200 pairs is very significant in Scottish population terms.

The kestrel is widely distributed in Dumfries and Galloway, Ayrshire and on the Clyde coast and is a common breeding species. There is a strong winter population, a point noted by Bannerman as early as the 1950s (Bannerman 1956): 'It is interesting to find that the kestrel population of southern Scotland is larger in winter than in summer'. Undoubtedly the southwest of Scotland, with a high percentage of unimproved sheep pasture characterising much of the upland, also supports a very high percentage of the Scottish population. In the Clyde area, increased sightings are attributed to a definite population increase since 1993 when systematic recording began with 30–60 pairs monitored. On the Isle of Arran, the population is stable at around 30 breeding pairs, the same number noted in a survey in the mid 1980s (Riddle 1986).

Although widespread in Argyll and Bute, the kestrel population is thin on the ground in an area largely dominated by buzzards. Coastal breeding sites are favoured and small populations exist on the main islands. Islay has 5–10 pairs, Bute 10–15 and Jura fewer than 5 pairs. On Mull, 80 home ranges were recorded as having been occupied at least once between 1991 and 2000 and the general picture seems to be one of numbers increasing. The Ross of Mull is particularly well populated. Almost all the nests are on crags, one in an old golden eagle nest, but there are no records as yet of pairs using old crow's nests. The pair using the eagle's nest was successful.

The situation on Mull is interesting as Graham (1890) describes the kestrel as by far the most abundant of 'the hawk tribe' there during the period 1852–1870, when it nested 'about on every precipitous sea cliff', a very similar pattern of nest choice to today's. The subsequent reduction has been attributed to the impoverishment of suitable foraging habitat due to the extensive re-afforestation programme and an increase in grazing pressure on grassland from a rise in deer numbers and domestic herbivores. Competition with the buzzard is also advanced as a factor (Rheinallt *et al.* 2007). The general picture seems to be one of the kestrel making a comeback.

Further north, Eigg supports six pairs and on Skye there seems to be a patchy distribution with the kestrel being more common in the north of the island and seemingly absent from the Cuillins range. Some of the smaller islands off the west coast, such as Canna, support 1–2 pairs which breed irregularly but Colonsay seems to be on the way up, with 4–5 pairs being recorded recently.

This review, albeit just for Scotland, does highlight the main factors affecting the changed status of the kestrel along with the fact that the picture is far from uniform across the country. The Argyll scenario encapsulates the main factors which are at play: land use changes affecting key habitats which are utilised by the kestrels for hunting, and an increase in competition due to the slow but welcome recovery of other raptor species.

The position in England as detailed in the most recent assessment by Rob Clements (2008) has parallels, not surprisingly, with the Scottish scene. Despite the steep decline in some parts of the country – much of northern and western England and large areas where there is intensive arable farming, such as Lincolnshire and parts of East Anglia – high densities of kestrels can be found in many parts of southern and central England, from South Yorkshire south to Dorset and east to Kent. He also alludes to competition and predation from the buzzard and goshawk as limiting factors. His most interesting assertion is that the current population is above 50,000 territorial pairs in Britain and that the most recent national assessments are underestimates, with some of the highest densities at 50+ pairs per hectad (10km × 10km square).

As my time monitoring the kestrel in Ayrshire conveniently overlaps with this seismic change in the status of this species, it is worth using the results over the past 35 years to examine these key factors in more detail. Does the data dovetail with the national scenario? Are there parallels elsewhere? Is there major cause for concern? What steps can be taken to help the kestrel, if it indeed needs help?

The small falcon strategy of high productivity and a quick turnover of population is certainly reflected in the Ayrshire figures. No matter the parameter, the outcome is impressive, especially brood survival which is exceptionally and consistently high. Once the kestrel pairs get young in the nest and see them over the first few critical days, a high percentage reach the flying stage.

*Productivity Summary 1979–2009*

| | |
|---|---|
| Average clutch size | 5 |
| % eggs hatched | 76 |
| Average number of young reared all attempts | 2.9 |
| Average number reared per successful attempt | 3.9 |
| % eggs from which young fledged | 73 |
| % brood survival | 90 |
| % breeding attempt successful | 75 |

The failure rate is highest at the pre-laying and clutch stages. First-year mortality is high after the young leave the parental influence and accounts for 60% of the ringing recoveries (see Chapter 1). Mortality rate decreases with birds which survive this initial hurdle.

*Breeding Failures 1979–2009 (787 results)*

| | | % |
|---|---|---|
| Pre Laying | 50 | 31 |
| Clutch | 108 | 61 |
| Brood | 21 | 8 |
| | | |
| Accident/Weather | 54 | 33 |
| Predation and Territorial Competition | 16 | 11 |
| Human Interference | 40 | 24 |
| Unkown | 54 | 32 |

This summary obviously does not tell the full story: it is much more complex when more flesh is put on the bones. First of all, let us separate out man's impact, both direct and indirect, before tackling the natural factors. When the figure relating to the percentage of human interference is broken down, the story is a very positive one.

At the end of the 1970s, the *Kes* effect was waning fast although there were still incidents where kestrels were taken by children as pets or for falconry. The days of children roaming the countryside looking for eggs or taking young from the nest are, quite simply, long gone. There is little appetite for this type of activity in the face of the huge range of alternative recreational activities available. The lure of sedentary activities fuelled by the explosion in information technology wins hands down. I would be very surprised if the Ayrshire figures are not a snapshot of what is happening countrywide. The telling statistic is that in the last ten years only four breeding failures were attributed to direct human interference in my study areas.

Even today the kestrel is caught up in the mindless killing of raptors and still features in the RSPB annual persecution roll call. One particular problem relates to cage traps used for catching crows and this has been the subject of a particular crusade for Dave Dick, the former Species Protection Officer with RSPB Scotland (Dick and Stronach 1999). Dave received several reports of the multiple trapping of kestrel family groups, mostly in the summer months after the young had fledged. These birds are not normally carrion eaters and are probably attracted by small birds or rodents feeding on grain, or insects and maggots produced from the carrion. Once a bird is trapped, the others are drawn in by its movements, along with a mixture of curiosity and family ties, and suffer the same fate. They cannot survive long periods without food and shelter and are liable to perish from hunger and exposure if not released relatively quickly.

Frustratingly, this problem can easily be overcome by discipline: regular visits, locking traps open when they are not in use and releasing non-target species like raptors. The Wildlife and Countryside Act (1981) makes it illegal to trap wild birds in Scotland and the UK, but

*Kestrels for Company*

*Cage traps pose a problem, with multiple catches a distinct possibility in late summer*

Open General Licences issued annually by the Government authorise the use of cage traps for catching certain species for certain purposes. Trap operators must comply with the conditions stated in the licence, including inspecting the traps daily at intervals of no more than 24 hours and removing any caught birds.

Even taking these facts into consideration, I would argue that in the big picture of raptor persecution the kestrel, with its few commercial conflicts with man, does not suffer badly at the direct hand of man.

By contrast, the way in which man manages the countryside, especially when large-scale changes occur, can influence food availability and determine the level of occupancy and productivity. The two best examples are agricultural intensification and afforestation. There is no doubt that changes in agricultural practices have led to the reduction of potential hunting areas for kestrels and a reduction in small mammals, a key component in their diet. Worryingly, a decline in meadow pipits, starlings and skylarks across the United Kingdom has been identified in the BTO's Breeding Bird Survey results. All these species feature as kestrel prey items, particularly in the latter part of the breeding cycle when inexperienced young songbirds can be an important element in the diet, especially in poor vole years.

The preferred prey item of the kestrel is the short-tailed field vole which thrives in rough, poorly-grazed and unimproved grassland. Agricultural intensification has resulted in heavier grazing pressure and pasture improvement which have combined to reduce vole habitat, especially through England and Wales, with less marked changes in Scotland. This has had a knock-on effect on kestrel breeding numbers. Mike Shrubb gives an excellent analysis of this in his book (Shrubb 1993).

The scene is ever-changing. The set-aside scheme, introduced in the early 1990s to aid the arable sector after the over-production of seed grain in Europe, came to an end in 2008 and was replaced by the Land Stewardship Scheme. The former – compulsory – scheme took arable land out of production and created, amongst other things, good vole habitat. Land has now gone back to production and the stewardship scheme with its environmental benefits has had less of a take-up.

As we saw before, the kestrel population in southwest Scotland is high compared with the rest of Scotland and a look at the Land Cover of Scotland map of 1998, produced by the Macaulay Land Use Research Institute, clearly shows the reason why. This area has a preponderance of grassland – uniform, good rough and poor rough – and a relatively small amount of arable land. Potentially it is one of the best areas for kestrels in Scotland. Local conditions do vary across the country and not all ground is best suited to the kestrel's needs.

My main study area on the Ayrshire border with Dumfries and Galloway is dominated by sheep-grazed rough pasture on the fringes of massive conifer cover which is moving into second rotation. The greatest concentration of upland planting with sitka spruce in Scotland was in the southwest, with a later switch to the peatlands of north Scotland in the late 1970s and early 1980s. Relatively little new commercial planting, apart from native woodland schemes, has taken place since the 1980s. Forestry Commission figures give a graphic account of the scale of the turnaround. In 1971 they planted 17,832 hectares of conifers in Scotland: in 2007 this had fallen to only seven hectares. By comparison, 5,440 hectares of felled woodland were replanted in 2007. This second rotation is not utilised by the kestrel to the same degree as the initial planting, possibly because the ground cover of felling debris does not provide the same open grassland regimes as afforded by the new-planted ground in the 1960s and early 1970s, and because there is much more cover for small mammals. The surrounding mature forestry now supports more large avian predators such as the goshawk, which preys on the kestrel.

As the forests matured the loss of hunting areas resulted in several of the early study area territories being deserted, engulfed by a sea of sitka. Kestrels did however use crows' nests on the forest edge if suitable hunting areas were within easy reach.

The habitat changes described above have affected the availability of short-tailed field voles, with a negative knock-on effect on kestrel numbers. In northern temperate latitudes, field vole populations are cyclical, reaching peaks every three to four years followed by a collapse in numbers and subsequent recovery to the next peak in a boom-and-bust pattern. These vole cycles do not occur synchronously across Scotland and some regions, such as the Highlands and some of the islands, have very low numbers of voles or even none at all.

There are records of severe vole plagues in the south of Scotland in 1875–1876 (Elliot 1878), 1891–1892 (Adair 1892 and Harvie Brown *et al.* 1893) and 1970–1972 (Mitchell *et al.* 1974). When this happens, kestrels and short-eared owls breed in large numbers, the kestrels often tolerating very close nesting in these times of plenty. In the plagues of 1888–1891, the number of voles was so great, and their impact on agricultural ground so disastrous, that the Board of Agriculture appointed a Departmental Committee to enquire into the causes. Interestingly, this was amongst the responses:

'Nearly every witness…giving it as his belief that the outbreak was due to the destruction of natural enemies of voles.'

*Above left: Typical habitat in study area: upland unimproved pasture and shelter belts*

*Above right: The planting of conifers in the 1970s was extensive and had a huge impact on kestrels*

*Below: The amount of ground cover at second-rotation stage is not as attractive to hunting birds*

One of the recommendations was that landowners should instruct their staff that owls, buzzards and kestrels were not to be destroyed.

George Bolan (1912) paints a vivid picture of just how spectacular the build-up of kestrels could be. In 1897, on a low range of crags at Craig Laigh, a few miles east of Haltwhistle, he found seven kestrel nests within 40 yards. When he checked the area he had no fewer than 13 adult kestrels hovering in the air above him, all calling at the same time.

The 20th century example was at Eskdalemuir where between 1965 and 1970, 6,800 hectares of former sheep range was afforested. In ideal conditions an abnormal increase in vole numbers occurred in 1971–1972 when vole-associated raptors cashed in. The numbers documented in 1972 were 12 pairs of kestrels, 14 pairs of short-eared owls, three pairs each of barn owl and long-eared owl and one pair of tawny owls: 33 pairs of raptors in a classic response to a glut of prey.

In more recent times the boom in vole numbers resulting from new forestry planting in an area of Dumfries and Galloway resulted in one crag having four pairs of kestrels nesting successfully in 1974 and six pairs in 1975. What a sight that must have been.

One of the great benefits of working with one species over a long period of time is that trends do become apparent. In terms of the relationship between kestrel productivity and vole numbers, a very definite pattern emerged. I worked closely with Geoff Shaw, whose barn owl study areas partly overlapped with the kestrel territories or were contiguous in other areas. Vole signs were monitored to assess the abundance of voles in March and April each year giving data on the peaks and troughs (Shaw and Riddle 2003).

Kestrel numbers peaked in the good vole years and normally declined steeply in the following year, as mentioned previously. The timing of the breeding cycle was strongly associated with vole numbers with large clutches being laid earlier in peak vole years.

If a vole peak and good weather coincide, then productivity can be very high. In 1997, for example, there was an unprecedented 18 clutches of six and one of seven. One clutch of eight

*Percentage of Kestrel territories occupied in southwest Scotland study area 1986–2009 (arrow = peak vole years)*

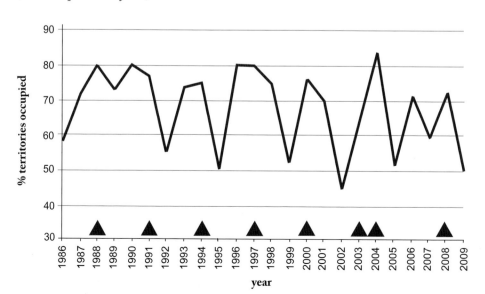

eggs during a vole peak was the highest recorded. A predominance of clutches of six eggs in a season is a very good indicator of a vole peak.

This very consistent link to vole cycles in the southwest of Scotland, with regular broods of five and six in peak years, is out of kilter with recent BTO figures. The kestrel has been put on the Nest Record Scheme Concern List (*BTO News* 267, 2006) because of the significant decline since the early 1990s suggesting that more pairs are rearing three chicks instead of four or five. The prevalence of grassland habitat in my study areas may well be the main factor in determining my higher figures.

*A rare clutch of eight eggs during a vole peak year*

*Change of kestrel brood size since 1966*

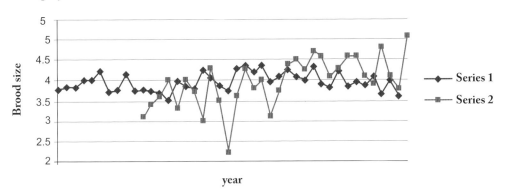

Series 1 – BTO figures  Series 2 – Ayrshire figures

An interesting footnote is provided by a graph (Petty *et al.* 2003) showing the kestrel decline in Kielder Forest as the goshawk population grew. What was also obvious from the figures was that even in the dramatic decline, the kestrels still peaked every few years, presumably in response to vole numbers.

Another land use factor which is literally on the horizon is the impact of wind farms on the kestrel. More and more terrestrial farms are coming online in Scotland and, as yet, very little work is being done post-commissioning to monitor raptor collisions. Only a trickle of data is coming through. At Braes of Doune in Stirlingshire, five kestrel carcasses have been found

Above: As yet, the full impact of wind farms on kestrel numbers is unknown

Below left: Kestrels are being found dead under turbines

184  Below right: This kestrel was literally cut in half

under the turbines and I have one record of a kestrel ringed at one of my sites being killed by a turbine three kilometres from its natal site on 27 September 2006, soon after fledging. Two of the Doune birds were also juveniles and this may be significant, as inexperience may be a contributory factor.

Certainly work done at Campo de Gibraltar in Spain in 1993 and 1994 found that kestrel deaths occurred during the peak annual abundance in summer. Carcasses, 36 in all, were found on open habitats round a single wind farm and the researchers concluded that the risk may have resulted from hunting habitat preferences on sparsely-vegetated areas (Barrios and Rodriguez 2004). Eight of the birds collected between 15 July and 17 August could be identified as juveniles. This site was not considered to be on a main migration route and the birds were assessed as being residents.

The most notorious windfarm complex is at Altmount Pass in California where the 5,400 turbines were built in 1982 along a major raptor migration route. An estimated 880–1,300 raptors, including hundreds of American kestrels, are killed there each year. The scale of the carnage is appalling and hopefully the environmental impact studies mandatory in this country will allow us to assess potential risks and avoid locating new farms in inappropriate sites.

Lack of data is obviously a problem in assessing the impact of wind turbines and this is compounded by the fact that scavengers may remove carcasses and distort the picture. Kestrels certainly seem to have no inhibitions about using wind farm environments. While carrying out fieldwork in the vicinity of turbines over a nine-day period, I watched kestrels regularly flying between active turbines and hunting in close proximity to them. Kevin Duffy also recorded two instances of kestrels perched on top of the aerials on turbines, although at a time when the blades were not spinning. It is certainly an area that needs much more attention.

Very worrying is the report by the Scottish Agricultural Science Agency's Wildlife Incident Scheme (Hartley *et al.* 2009) which states that of 17 dead kestrels tested for anti-coagulant residues between 2003 and 2009, 47% were positive (buzzard 48% of 290 tested, red kite 78% of 63 tested). It is also suggested that 38% of the kestrels tested had levels of rodenticides which were classed at the "at risk" level. This is of very serious concern, indicating a high level of rodenticide use in the countryside and an obvious lack of compliance under the Control of Pesticides Regulations 1986. The sample sizes may be small but the warnings are there. Further research is needed to clarify that this is not a major factor in the decline of the kestrel in Scotland: surely we are not revisiting the bad old days of the 1960s and 1970s?

Although man's hand can be seen in many aspects of the lives of kestrels, there are still very influential natural factors at work: the weather, competition for territories and nest sites, predation and, as described above, vole cycles. Any of these can dictate the outcome of a breeding season. Weather is a critical factor which can affect the timing of the breeding cycle, productivity and juvenile survival in the first winter, as the Ayrshire data illustrates.

The timing of the onset of laying has a significant effect upon productivity. Early breeders which laid in April had larger clutches than those pairs which began laying in May, and early breeders produced more fledged young, a trend which has also been recorded in Holland (Cavé 1968). Other studies (Dijkstra *et al.* 1982 and Village 1986) also found that clutch size declined with the advance in the laying date and that females laid at earlier dates in high vole years compared to low vole years. Inclement weather such as snow, rain and low temperatures can delay the start of the cycle while open, warm springs can advance breeding attempts. Cavé also showed by experimentation that low temperatures in spring resulted in the female kestrel having less energy available for the formation of eggs. Rainfall inhibits the hunting activity of kestrels and the above-ground activity of voles so weather can play a major role in the timing.

In a study area between Cologne and Bonn on the west side of the River Rhine, Kostrzewa and Kostrzewa (1990) also found that the weather was a key factor. The density of territorial pairs was dependent upon rainfall in the pre-laying period in March and April and the number of young fledged per successful pair was highly correlated with May and June temperatures.

The benefits of breeding early are clear: to have young in the nest at the time of maximum food availability in May and June and ensuring that the fledged young have as much time as possible to build reserves and hone their hunting skills before the first real crunch of winter hits in November and December.

Consistent spells of good and bad weather have over the years regularly influenced the outcome of breeding seasons. Here are a few examples from the Ayrshire study:

1984

Superb summer, sunshine all the way: 94% of eggs hatched, 83% of eggs laid resulted in flying young, laying dates in April. 3.7 young produced per breeding attempt.

1985

Dry start to the season, little rainfall, high occupation: average clutch size 5.2, then weather change. Very wet late spring and summer, only 68% of eggs hatched, brood sizes reduced and some complete failures at the brood stage.

1986

The wettest season on record with only 58% of territories occupied: an average clutch size of 4.3, only 35% of eggs hatched and a miserly 1.3 young reared per breeding attempt. Most pairs did not begin to breed until May and one pair started on 1 June, the latest on record. Seven out of 8 failures were due to desertion at the clutch stage.

1987

Early season weather excellent: clutch size average 5.3, then wet and cold conditions in June resulted in depletion at the brood stage.

1991

Two critical spells of poor weather dictated the outcome of the season, two weeks in early April and three weeks in June. Cold, wet and windy conditions initially inhibited breeding and then caused depletion in broods. Five pairs reared single chicks, a very unusual occurrence and this in a high vole year.

1992

Up until the second week in May it looked as if the season would rival 1986: only 12 out of 33 territories checked were occupied and only four clutches recorded. The weather had been consistently windy and cold. Transformation to sunny dry weather which prevailed almost unchanged until the end of the season. Within four days, between 20 and 24 May, 14 more hens started to breed.

1993

Torrential rain from 13 to 18 May caused 11 pairs to desert – sites totally waterlogged.

Normally the kestrel is very resilient and can cope well with mixed weather conditions but the seven seasons illustrated above show just what an impact both adverse and benign conditions can have on the outcome, even when food supplies are plentiful.

One of the main thrusts of the kestrel work has been the ringing programme (see Chapter 1) and once again the weather comes into play. Ringing recoveries do illustrate the difficulty of survival of first-year birds with 55% being found dead in the first autumn and winter. Cavé's figure for mortality of young birds in their first year was 51%. Many of the birds found dead were reported as being in very poor condition and those handed in to rescue centres were normally exhausted or very lightweight. In late July and August 1998, 17 young kestrels in very poor condition were handed in to Hessilhead Wildlife Rescue Trust, Ayrshire during a spell of particularly stormy unseasonable weather. Three birds from one brood in Ayrshire, recovered within a few days of each other at Newbury, Guernsey and King's Lynn, had flown almost exactly the same distance and succumbed in severe weather in November. Cavé also found that the survival figure was higher for early fledged young and lower for those which fledged late. The advantages of early fledging is that the young birds have more time to gain resources and experience in hunting before the severe winter weather hits home.

The recent welcome recovery of raptors has seen a major shift in the kestrel's status in relation to other species, as was graphically illustrated in Chapter 7. The fall in percentage terms from 65% to 28% is a very significant reduction. What we are probably seeing is a readjustment as competition for food and nest sites, plus predation from larger species, virtually absent in the 1960s and 1970s, restores a more natural order.

A look at a selection of kestrel territories in Ayrshire is indicative of the numerical changes in species. In the early days of monitoring, the kestrel was the only avian predator in most small upland shelter belts. Now these territories are more crowded with ravens, buzzards and barn owls, and the element of competition for food and nest sites, along with the inevitable increase in daily interaction, must be having an effect.

*Kestrels Ayrshire Raptor Recovery*

|  | 1987 | 1997 | 2007 |
|---|---|---|---|
| V Wood | K | K | BZ |
| H Wood | K | K BO | K BO |
| D Hill | K | K | K BZ RN |
| K Farm | K | K LEO BZ | K BZ |
| M2 | K | K BO | BZ |
| C Quarry | K | K BO | K BO RN BZ |
| M Head | K | K BO | K BO RN |
| S Wood | K | K | BO |
| M5 | K | K BO | BZ BO |
| G Shaw | K | K | K BO BZ |

K – kestrel, BO – barn owl, LEO – long-eared owl, BZ – buzzard, RN – raven

The most obvious incomer is the buzzard. When I first moved to south Ayrshire in 1972, there were only two small areas in the county in which to see buzzards. In *The Birds of Ayrshire* (Paton and Pike 1929) this species is described as one of the rarest in the county. Now the buzzard is established everywhere and is the raptor you are most likely to encounter – a very healthy situation, I hasten to add. In the face of competition from the dominant and very territorial buzzard, the kestrel probably just moves out of the nesting territory. There can be no doubt that the buzzard takes the kestrel as prey and there is plenty of anecdotal evidence that this happens.

*Early indications are that buzzards do impact negatively on kestrels*

A member of the Lothian and Borders Raptor Study Group, John Pringle, sent me details of a kestrel being killed by a buzzard which was hunting the same slopes with its mate. The female kestrel dropped down towards an intended prey, closely followed by one of the buzzards which came up carrying the kestrel. After some close flying, the prey was passed in midair to the other buzzard which settled down and fed on the kestrel. Bob Swann recorded a failed kestrel breeding attempt at the mid-brood stage at a nest 500 metres from a regular buzzard nest. The plucked remains of the female kestrel were found on the buzzard's nest.

By far the most bizarre sighting came from Chris Rollie as he drove one day through a kestrel territory in southwest Scotland. A buzzard flew low over the road, clutching an adult kestrel in its talons, only to be badly distracted when it nearly collided with the car windscreen. The buzzard released its victim which made the most of its opportunity and escaped.

Shrubb (2003) and Green (2002) also implicate the expanding buzzard population in the decline of the kestrel in Wales, citing competition for food as the reason. Provisional buzzard and kestrel maps for the 2008–2011 Bird Atlas in the Fife area show a marked decrease in kestrel distribution since the fieldwork for the Fife Atlas in the late 1990s, with a correspondingly marked increase in buzzard distribution.

One very interesting development is on the Isle of Colonsay where for many years – in seven out of the 17 years between 1988 and 2004 – one pair of kestrels intermittently bred. The situation improved at the same time as a second pair of golden eagles started breeding successfully. From 2005 to 2009 the number of kestrel pairs holding territory rose from two to four. Simultaneously the buzzard status on the island changed. Although the number of occupied territories remained the same, subtle changes began to be noticed: single birds in residence, nests in less open, obvious locations, evidence of predation of buzzards by the eagles, and buzzards avoiding prominent landscape features, almost adopting a much lower profile. Further monitoring and analysis of the interaction between the raptor species and the effects of the population dynamics could be very revealing.

The kestrel is particularly vulnerable to attack due to its hovering mode of hunting, making it easy prey as it concentrates on the ground below in a more or less stationary position. The goshawk situation in Ayrshire and the Keilder Forest has already been covered in Chapter 2. The extent of the removal of other raptors from the wooded areas in which the goshawk settles must not be understated as the impact locally can be severe. The kestrel population in the Netherlands is reported to have halved since 1990 and an increase in goshawks is put forward as one reason for the decline (Bijlsma 1999).

There are also parallels with the American kestrel (*Falco spaverius*). Populations of the larger Cooper's hawk (*Accipiter cooperii*) which has increased in the northeast and other regions in the USA between 1974 and 2004 may have contributed to kestrel declines, since studies at Hawk Mountain and elsewhere have demonstrated that this species regularly preys upon American kestrels and can become habituated to hunting at kestrel nest boxes (Dr. C. J. Farmer and J. P. Smith 2009).

The relationship between the peregrine falcon and the kestrel is a fascinating one. The peregrine does prey on kestrels and remains are regularly found in nests and on plucking posts. On four occasions in the southwest of Scotland, however, peregrine pairs have taken over kestrel nests after losing their own clutches and on two occasions actually reared broods of four and two kestrels (Ratcliffe 1980). It is not known if the peregrines killed the kestrel adults but it would not be a surprise if they had.

In most of the traditional cliff nest sites which have been reclaimed by the peregrine as it has recovered in numbers, the kestrel which had taken advantage of the other bird's absence is not tolerated. There are always exceptions to the rule, though, and in one remarkable instance in Devon in 2006 the nest scrapes were only six metres or so apart on a cliff face. The nests were just out of sight of each other round a rocky corner. The chicks from the two broods, five kestrels and two peregrines, appeared to accept each other and mingled on the ledges on two occasions. Phil Johnson, who was monitoring the site, saw young kestrels begging for food from the female peregrine as she approached with prey. Incredibly, the female 'appeared to

189

READJUSTMENT

make no distinction between the visiting youngsters and her own and did her best to feed the lot'. (*British Birds* Notes 2008).

As well as suffering from the disadvantage of being easy to kill, the kestrel also has the occasional problem of dealing with owls. Barn owls and tawny owls do compete with the kestrel for nest sites, especially in buildings or for nest boxes. In one site in the Ayrshire study area, the towers of the Dams, barn owls have on three occasions taken over kestrel nest sites when the kestrels were on full clutches. The barn owls then laid clutches nearby and reared young. The obvious advantage that the owls enjoy in a conflict situation is that they can operate in both daylight and darkness – a telling bonus.

In all cases I have recorded, the kestrel comes off second best to the barn owl when there is negative interaction. Yet, just like the case with the peregrine, there are examples of the barn owl and kestrel co-existing in close proximity in adjacent holes in trees, in hay sheds, on cliff sites and in buildings.

Brian Little told me that in 1956, while raking round in Gosforth Park, Northumberland, looking for sparrowhawk nests, he disturbed a long-eared owl which came off an old crow's nest in an oak tree. On climbing the tree, he found three long-eared owl eggs and four fresh kestrel eggs: the kestrel pair had been presumably been displaced. A later visit revealed one newly-hatched kestrel and the remaining six eggs. Sadly, what would have been a remarkable story ended with the young kestrel chicks being eaten and the owlets surviving. Brian also recorded a kestrel female as prey at a tawny owl nest box in Kielder Forest in 2010.

A closer look at the relationship between tawny owls and kestrels illustrates just how much we still have to learn. Until I discussed the matter in detail with Steve Petty, who since the late 1970s has been extensively monitoring the tawny owl populations in Keilder, I had no conception of the possibility of tawny owls having any significant effect on kestrels.

*Barn owl pellets beside a failed clutch of kestrel eggs*

*The shattered remains of a kestrel chick taken by a golden eagle*

However, Steve has recorded five kestrels being taken as prey by tawny owls (Petty 1999), their remains being found either in the owl box or within 50 metres of an occupied box. There is no direct proof but Steve suspects that they take them out at night near or at kestrels' nests. He also recorded an incident in 1985 involving the killing of both a female sparrowhawk and female kestrel by a tawny owl on a small sandstone crag at the edge of the forest. At least two of the ledges had been used by breeding kestrels in the past and after a tawny owl started to nest on the cliff, the plucked remains of the sparrowhawk and kestrel were found close to the owl's nest.

During his study of the sparrowhawks in Keilder in the 1970s and 1980s, most of the sparrowhawk nests he was monitoring came under attack from tawny owls at some time during the period they were occupied. Most hawk nests survived these attacks but some nests failed.

I recorded a kestrel laying two eggs on a coastal cliff nest (*Seasons with the Kestrel* p. 75) only for a tawny owl pair to take over, lay two eggs and rear two owlets. The fate of the kestrels was unknown. Steve is working on a monograph of the tawny owl and it should make fascinating reading.

Even the mighty golden eagle will take kestrels and in Ayrshire, where eagle density is extremely low, kestrel feathers have been found in an eyrie. There are numerous examples from golden eagle enthusiasts, such as the late Lea MacNally and Jeff Watson, of kestrel remains at eagle nests. On Mull, where there is a strong coastal population of kestrels, resident golden eagles hunt them, especially when the young and inexperienced birds are in the air. The Lakeland eagles were also partial to kestrels. Dave Walker recorded sixteen kestrels taken as prey, including one instance where the kestrel adult was killed by an eagle, plucked and then abandoned. The nestlings were then removed, farmed one by one from the nest, and taken to feed the eaglet. What will happen if the eagle owl becomes established?

So, in summary, the kestrel is in decline with a population in the United Kingdom of between 35,000 and 50,000. Its conservation status is amber, indicating a population decline of between 25% and 49% which is of medium conservation concern. Recently the kestrel has joined the concern list in the BTO's Nest Record Scheme due to a significant decline in brood size and Breeding Bird Surveys results have shown extensive declines over the UK.

1. The European conservation status of the kestrel is category SPEC3, an unfavourable category with an overall population of between 300,000 and 444,000 pairs (see Appendix 1). We do not have definite answers as to why the decline is happening, but it is probably due to a combination of factors affecting the distribution and productivity of the kestrel – a mixture of man-made and natural. Habitat changes in their favoured grassland environment due to agricultural intensification, along with a reduction in new planting in the forestry field have reduced foraging areas and therefore food availability, primarily small mammals. A reduction in the populations of passerine prey species such as meadow pipits, skylarks and starlings may also be a contributory factor.

2. Competition and predation as a result of the slow but steady recovery of the country's raptor population, along with the vagaries of the weather, are key natural factors. A worrying trend is the high levels of rodenticides being found in dead kestrels and although the sample size is small, it cannot be dismissed and may be playing a part in the recent decline of the kestrel in Scotland.

3. The picture is far from uniform across the United Kingdom, with the kestrel doing well in certain areas and poorly in others. In southern Scotland and southern and central parts of England, for example, the kestrel is easily holding its own while in much of northern and western England, Lincolnshire and parts of east Ayrshire, Wales, Ireland and the Highlands of Scotland the kestrel is definitely in decline.

4. In order to assess the true picture and take steps, if necessary, to improve its conservation status, there needs to be better coverage and more robust data. At present the data is fragmented across the country so an increase in fieldwork is needed. There has never been a national survey of kestrels as species such as the hen harrier, peregrine and golden eagle have been a priority. The figures in the 2008 Scottish Raptor Monitoring Scheme Report emphasise poor recording of home ranges compared with other species: 597 peregrine, 310 golden eagle, 421 hen harrier and a meagre 115 kestrel. There are obvious difficulties in conducting a national survey: the kestrel is not sedentary and its response to fluctuating food supplies means that there is irregular spacing of pairs and variation in occupancy from year to year. If a survey had taken place in 2000, for example, the results would have been very positive for Ayrshire in a peak vole year. In 2005, though, territorial occupation was only 51% when vole numbers bottomed out. A further complication is that vole cycles are not synchronous across the UK. The *Bird Atlas* 2007–2011 results will give us a clearer picture of the most recent trends.

5. We need to evaluate as a matter of urgency the true impact on the kestrel of the recovery of other raptors. In an ever-changing environment we are at present in a transitional period. A natural readjustment may very well be taking place as raptors in the UK are recovering from a low period in their history caused by a combination of pesticides, persecution and changes in land use. Perversely the kestrel, with few direct conflicts with man and little competition in avian terms, prospered in favourable conditions such as when new forestry plantations mushroomed across the country. We may have to temper our view of the decline of the kestrel and accept that the readjustment will stabilise when species reach their carrying capacity in the

countryside. This may still take some time as many species are still under pressure from persecution.

6. No one knows what direction will be taken by key land uses such as agriculture, with its strong links to subsidies, or forestry, in terms of new planting, and how they will impact on the grassland habitats on which the kestrel forages and thrives. It should be a priority to address the problem of overgrazing and subsequent loss of foraging ground and encouragement should be given to creating a mosaic of land use, including the maintenance of a percentage of rough, unmanaged grassland. The positive example in Orkney quoted earlier is the kind of kestrel-friendly agri-environment scheme which should be encouraged. The effect of windfarms is far from clear and more investigative work is needed.

7. Further research is needed to assess both the scale and impact of the misuse of rodenticides in the countryside which may be a contributory factor in the kestrel's decline in Scotland. Comparison with recent residue level trends in England, where the Breeding Bird Survey does not show the same decline, would help to shed light on the situation.

8. Species plans in Local Biodiversity Action Plans can encourage nest box schemes where nest sites are lacking, and kestrel-friendly mowing in open spaces like parks and golf courses can improve the habitat for small mammals. The Hawk and Owl Trusts network of nest box schemes and their Kestrel Highway Project sre exemplars of this.

9. Protective legislation in both Europe and the UK is good but needs to be implemented more effectively. An understanding of the role of raptors in rural economics and a better- informed and supportive general public will hopefully accelerate the gradual erosion of the antiquated anti-raptor culture.

10. We need to keep our finger on the pulse not simply by staying vigilant to the kestrel's position but also by maintaining a high profile, allowing positive conservation action to be taken if necessary. This book is part of that effort.

I do detect some encouraging green shoots in the kestrel world. Strategic population monitoring in Ireland began in 2010 to establish a baseline database on the status, distribution and ecology of the kestrel, driven by John Lusby of Birdwatch Ireland. A 'Concise Species Action Plan' is in the process of being produced by the RSPB. The kestrel is now featuring in the Scottish Raptor Monitoring Group discussions following the BTO figures. A forestry Commission nest box scheme is planned for 2012 in my local area and Dave Anderson and his team have a scheme up and running in the Stirling area. All initiatives going in the right direction.

Finally, we must not forget that this small falcon has an excellent response capability and is well- equipped to exploit favourable conditions quickly and to the full by producing large clutches and broods. It is able to breed in its first year and will tolerate close neighbours in food surplus years. The kestrel's mobility and catholic lifestyle allow it to ride out even poor years by diversifying its prey range.

I am glad to have been involved with the kestrel for the last four decades but have slight pangs for the pre-statistics pioneer days of Seton Gordon, although I would have struggled to live with the levels of persecution and the mindset of landowners. I hope the inevitable technical advances will not diminish the detective element which the raptor worker enjoys so much.

The kestrel's lifestyle stands it in good stead and despite the pressures upon it, I would be surprised if it does not continue to thrive in our towns and countryside, even if in smaller numbers. The kestrel is, if nothing else, a great survivor. I have heard the merlin described as the Jack Russell of the raptor world and I would say that the kestrel comes from the same mould. To see a pair of kestrels in suicide mode, nipping at the tail of a hen goshawk in her own territory in the face of superior size and power, sums up for me the character of this superb little falcon.

This was reinforced while on holiday on the Isle of Canna in 2010. A golden eagle had drifted inland from the coast and landed on a ridge. The challenge was immediately taken up by the pair of resident kestrels as they mobbed the eagle, continuously diving and veering off, causing the much larger raptor to duck. By luck I had the glasses trained on the scene at the very moment when the male kestrel actually clipped the head of the eagle with its talons, just like a Plains Indian counting coup on his foe. Magnificent.

*The kestrel has the potential to bounce back, thanks to its catholic lifestyle*

# References and further reading

## Chapter 1

Bijlsma, R.G. 2007. Trends and Breeding Performance of Raptors in the Netherlands in 2006. *De Takkeling* 12 (1): 7–55.

Chough Nest Boxes. *BTO News,* May–June 2008, pp. 16 and 17.

Couzens, D. 2007. Secret Lives of Common Birds. *Bird Watching,* September 2007, pp. 46–51.

Hardey, J., Crick, H.Q.P., Wernham, C.V., Riley, H., Etheridge, B. and Thompson, D. 2006. *Raptors: a Field Guide to Survey and Monitoring.* HMSO, Edinburgh.

Korpimaki, E., Hakkarainen, H., Laaksonen, T. & Vasko, V. 2008. *Scottish Birds* 28: 19–27.

Riddle, G.S. 1985. Kestrels Attending Oil Installations in the North Sea. *North Sea Bird Club Report:* 63–70.

Three species 'Hot Bed' in A-frame Nest Box. *Peregrine,* Spring 2008.

Tinbergen, L. 1940. Beobachtungen über die Arbeitsteiling des Turmfalken (*Falco Tinnunculus*) wahrend der Fortpflanzungszeit. Ardea 29: 63–98.

## Chapter 2

Balfour, E. 1955. Kestrels Nesting on the Ground in Orkney. *Bird Notes,* 26: 245–253.

Hedges, J.W. 1984. *Tomb of the Eagles: a Window on Stone Age Tribal Britain.* John Murray (Publishers) Ltd.

Petty, S.J. *et al.* 2003. The Decline of Common Kestrels *Falco Tinnunculus* in a Forested Area of Northern England: the Role of Predation by Northern Goshawks *Accipter Gentilis. Ibis,* 145: 472–483.

## Chapter 3

Cavé, A.J. 1968. The Breeding of the Kestrel *Falco tinnunculus (L.)* in the reclaimed area Oostelijk Flevoland. *Arch. néerl. Zool.* 18: 313–407.

Collar, N.J., Stuart, S.N. 1985. Threatened Birds of Africa and Related Islands. *ICBP/IUCN Red Data Book.* International Council for Bird Preservation and International Union for Conservation of Nature and Natural Resources, Cambridge.

Gaymer, R., Blackman, R. A. A., Dawson, P.G., Penny, M.J., Penny, C.M. 1969. *The Endemic Birds of Seychelles. Ibis,* 111, 157–176.

Gerlach, J. 2008. Seychelles Kestrel *Falco araea.* Arkive.

Groombridge, J.J., Bruford, M.W., Jones, C.G., Nicols, R.A. 2001. Estimating the Severity of the Population Bottleneck in the Mauritius Kestrel *Falco Punctatus* from Ringing Records Using MCMC Estimation. *Journal of Animal Ecology,* 70: 401–409.

Groombridge, J.J., Dawson, D.A., Burke, T., Prys-Jones, R., Brooke, M. D., Shah, N. 2009. Evaluating the demographic history of the Seychelles Kestrel *Falco Araea*: Genetic Evidence for Recovery from a Population Bottleneck Following Minimal Conservation Management. *Biological Conservation* 142: 2250–2257.

Jones, C.G., Heck, W., Lewis, R.E., Mungroo, Y., Slade, G., Cade, T.J. 1995. The Restoration of the Mauritius Kestrel *Falco Punctatus* Population. *Ibis,* 137–180.

Jones, C.G. and Owadally, A.W. 1985. The Status, Ecology and Conservation of the Mauritius Kestrel. ICBP Technical Publication 5, 1985.

Newton, E. 1867. On the Land-Birds of the Seychelles Archipelago. Ibis (2) 3: 335-360.

Riddle, G. 1992. *Seasons with the Kestrel.* Blandford, London.

Skerret, A., Bullock, I., and Disley, T. 2001. *Birds of Seychelles.* Helm Field Guides.

Watson, J. 1981. Population Ecology, Food and Conservation of the Seychelles Kestrel *Falco araea* on Mahé. Unpubl. PhD thesis. Aberdeen University.

Watson, J. 1992. Nesting Ecology of the Seychelles Kestrel *Falco Araea* on Mahé, Seychelles. *Ibis* 134, 259–267.

## Chapter 4

Bannerman, D.A. & Bannerman, W.M. 1965. History of the Birds of the Cape Verde Islands. *Birds of the Atlantic Islands*, Vol. 4. Oliver & Boyd, Edinburgh.

Hazevoet, C.J. 1995. *The Birds of the Cape Verde Islands.* British Ornithologists' Union, Dorchester.

Hille, S. and Winkler, H., 2000. Ecomorphology of Island Populations of the Kestrel *Falco Tinnunculus* on Cape Verde: 729–735 in R.D. Chancellor and B.U. Mayburg (Eds.), *Raptors at Risk.* World Working Group on Birds of Prey and Owls. Hancock Harse, Blaine, MN, USA.

Hille *et al.* 2003. Genetic Structure of Kestrel Populations and Colonisation of the Cape Verde Archipelago. *Molecular Ecology* 12: 2145–2151.

Ontiveras, D. 2005. Abundance and Diet of Alexander's Kestrel *Falco Tinnunculus Alexandri* on Boavista Island. (Archipelago of Cape Verde). *Journal of Raptor Research.* 39(1): 82–85.

## Chapter 6

Shaw, G. & Riddle, G. 2003. Comparative Responses of Barn Owls *Tyto Alba* and Kestrel *Falco Tinnunculus* to Vole Cycles in Southwest Scotland. *Birds of Prey in a Changing Environment.* 7: 131–136. HMSO.

## Chapter 7

Amar, A., Redpath, S. & Thirgood, S. 2003. Evidence for Food Limitation in the Declining Hen Harrier Population on the Orkney Islands, Scotland. *Biological Conservation,* 111, 377–384.

Banks A.N., Coombes, R.H. & Crick, H.Q.P. 2003. The Peregrine Falcon Breeding Population of the UK and Isle of Man in 2002. *BTO Research Report* 330. BTO, Thetford.

Bibby, J., Burgess, N.D. and Hill, D.A. 1992. *Bird Census Techniques.* BTO, RSPB. Academic Press.

Bird, D.M. and Bildstein, K.L. 2007. *Raptor Research and Management Techniques.* Hancock House Publishers.

Clements, R. 2002. The Common Buzzard in Britain: a New Population Estimate. *British Birds,* 95: 377–383.

Concern – the Red Kite *Milvus Milvus. Biological Conservation* 2010, doi: 10.1016/j.biocon.2010.02.002.

Crick, H.Q.P. & Ratcliffe, D.A. 1995. The Peregrine *Falco Peregrinus* Breeding Population of the United Kingdom in 1991. *Bird Study,* 42: 1–19.

Dennis, R. 2008. *A Life of Ospreys.* Whittles Publishing.

Dickie, I., Hughes, J. and Estaban, A. 2006. *Watched Like Never Before ... The Local Economic Benefits of Spectacular Bird Species.* RSPB, Scotland.

Eaton, M.A., Dillon, I.A., Stirling-Aird, P.K., Whitfield, D.P. 2007. The Status of the Golden Eagle *Aquila Chrysaetos* in Britain in 2003. *Bird Study,* 54, 212–220.

Gilbert, G., Gibbons, D.W. & Evans, J. 1998. *Bird Monitoring Methods.* RSPB.

Green R.E. 1996. The Status of the Golden Eagle in Britain in 1992. *Bird Study,* 43: 20–27.

Hardey, J., Crick, H.Q.P., Wernham, C.V., Riley, H., Etheridge, B and Thompson, D. 2006. *Raptors: a Field Guide to Survey and Moitoring.* HMSO, Edinburgh.

Haworth, P.F. & Fielding, A.H. 2009. *An Assessment of Woodland Habitat Utilisation by Breeding Hen Harriers.* Report to SNH (Project No. 24069) by Haworth Conservation, Isle of Mull.

Love, J.A. 1983. *The Return of the Sea Eagle.* Cambridge University Press.

Marquiss, M. (in press) 'The Goshawk' in Eds. Francis, I. & Cook, M. *North-East Scotland Breeding Bird Atlas 2002–2006.*

Ratcliffe, D.A. 1980. *The Peregrine Falcon.* Poyser, Calton.

Rebecca, G. & Bainbridge, I. 1998. The Breeding Status of the Merlin *Falco Columbaruis* in Britain in 1993–1994. *Bird Study,* 45: 172–187.

Scott, D. 2008. *Harriers' Journeys Around the World.* Tiercel Publishing.

*Scottish Bird Report* 1972. Scottish Ornithologists' Club.

The Scottish Government. *Bird Poisoning Hotspot Maps in Scotland, 2005–2009.* PAW Scotland 2010.

Scottish Office 1998. *Counting the Cost: The Continuing Persecution of Birds of Prey in Scotland.* The Scottish Office, Edinburgh.

Sim, I.M.W., Dillon, I.A., Eaton, M.A., Etheridge, B., Lindley, P., Riley, H., Saunders, R., Sharpe, C. and Tucker, M. 2007. Status of the Hen Harrier *Circus Cynaneus* in the UK and the Isle of Man in 2004, and a Comparison with the 1988–1989 and the 1998 Surveys. *Bird Study,* 54, 256–267.

Smart, J., Amar, A., Sim, I.M.W., Etheridge, B., Cameron, D., Christie, G. & Wilson, J.D. 2010. Illegal Killing Slows Population Recovery of a Re-Introduced Raptor of High Conservation Concern – The Red Kite Milvus milvus.

Sutherland, W.J., Newton, I and Green, R.E. 2004. *Bird Ecology and Conservation. A Handbook of Techniques.* Oxford University Press.

Whitfield, D.P., Fielding, A.H. and Whitehead, S. 2008. *A Conservation Framework for the Golden Eagle: Implications for the Conservation and Management of Golden Eagles in Scotland.* Scottish Natural Heritage-commissioned Report 193, Perth.

Chapter 8

Adair, P. 1892. The Short-eared Owl and the Kestrel in the Vole Plague districts. *Ann. Scot. Nat. Hist.,* 12: 219–231.

Amar, A., Arroyo, B., Meek, E., Redpath, S. & Riley, H. 2008. *Influence of Habitat on Breeding Performance of Hen Harriers (Circus Cyaneus) in Orkney. Ibis* 150: 400–404.

Baillie, S.R., Crick, H.Q.P., Balmer, D.E., Bashford, R.I., Beavan, L.P., Freeman, S.N., Marchant, J.H., Noble, D.G., Raven, M.J., Siriwardena, G.M., Thewlis, R., and Wernham, C.V. 2001. *Breeding Birds in the Wider Countryside: Their Conservation Status 2000.* Research Report 252. BTO, Thetford.

Balfour, E., 1955. *Kestrels Nesting on the Ground in Orkney.* Bird Notes 26: 245-53.

Bannerman, D.A., 1956. *The Birds of the British Isles, Vol. 5.* Oliver & Boyd, Edinburgh and London.

Barrios, L., and Rodriguez, A. 2004. Behavioural and environmental correlates of soaring – bird mortality at on shore wind turbines. *Journal of Applied Ecology* 41: 72–81.

Bijlsma, R.G., 1999. Trends and breeding sucess of raptors in the Netherlands in 1998. *De Takkeling.* 7 : 6-51

Bolan, G. 1912. *The Birds of Northumberland and the Eastern Borders.* Henry Hunter Blair, Alnwick.

Booth, C.J. 2000. *The Decline of the Kestrel as a Breeding Species in Orkney 1970–1999.* Orkney Bird Report. 1999: 90-93.

*British Birds* Notes. Peregrine Falcons feeding common kestrel chicks. *British Birds* 101. June 2008 p. 327.

Canham, M. 2003. *Raptor Monitoring in Highland and West Moray.* Highland Raptor Study Report 2003.

Cavé, A.J., 1968. The Breeding of the Kestrel *Falco tinnunculus (L.)* in the reclaimed area Oostelijk Flevoland. *Arch. néerl. Zool.* 18 : 313-407.

Clements, R. 2008. The Common Kestrel Population in Britain. *British Birds* 101: 228–234.

Coombes, R.H., Crowe, O., Lauder, A., Lysaght, L., O'Brien, C., O'Halloran, J., O'Sullivan, O., Tierney, T.D., Walsh, A.J., and Wilson, H.J. 2009. *Countryside Bird Survey Report* 1998–2007. Bird Watch Ireland, Wicklow.

Dick, D., and Stronach, A. 1999. The use, abuse and misuse of crow traps in Scotland: a report on behalf of the Scottish Raptor Study Groups and the RSPB. *Scottish Birds,* 2006–13.

Dijkstra, C., Vvursteen, L., Daan, S. & Masman, D. 1982. Clutch size and laying data in the Kestrel *Falco tinnunculus* : effect of supplementary food. *Ibis* 124: 210–213.

Dymond, J.N. 1991. *The Birds of Fair Isle.* Privately published.

Elkins, N., Reid, J.B. Brown, A.W., Robertson, D.G. & Smout, A.M. 2003. *The Fife Bird Atlas.* Woodland Studios, Dunfermline.

Elliot, Sir W. 1878. Some account of the plague of Field Mice in the border farms in 1876–1877. *Proc. Berw. Nat. Club,* 8: 447–472.

Farmer, C.J. & Smith J.P. 2009. Migration Monitoring Indicates Widespread Declines of American Kestrels (*Falco sparverius*) in North America. *J. Raptor Res.* 43 (4): 263–273.

Forrester, R.W., Andrews, I.J., McInerney, C.J., Murray, R.D., McGowan, R.Y., Zonfrillo, B., Betts, M.W., Jardine, D.C. & Grundy, D.S. 2007. *The Birds of Scotland.* SOC, Aberlady.

Francis, J., and Cook, M. (Eds.) 2011. *The Breeding Birds of North East Scotland.*

Gibbons, D.W., Reid, J.B. & Chapman, R.A. 1993. *The New Atlas of Breeding Birds in Britain and Ireland 1988–1991.* Poyser, London.

Graham, H.D. 1980. *The Birds of Iona and Mull, 1852–1870.* David Douglas, Edinburgh.

Green, J. 2002. *Birds in Wales 1992–2000.* Welsh Ornithological Society.

Hartley, G., Taylor, M. & Grifiths, C. 2009. Campaign Against Accidental and Illegal Poisoning (CAIP) Background Information SASA. November 2009.

Harvie-Brown, J.A., Trail, J.W.H. and Eagle Clarke, W. (Eds.) 1893. Report on the Plague of Field Voles in Scotland. *Ann. Scot. Nat. Hist.* 13: 129–145.

Hines, B. 1969. *A Kestrel for a Knave.* Penguin Books.

Kostrzewa, A., and Kostrzewa, R. 1990. The relationship of spring and summer weather with density and breeding performance of the Buzzard *Buteo buteo,* Goshawk *Accipiter gentiles* and Kestrel *Falco tinnunculus. Ibis.* 132: 515–524.

Leach, D., Barimore, C., and Crick, H. 2006. N.R.S. Concern List – five new species added. *BTO News*, 2006 November–December 4-5.

Mead, C. 2000. *The State of the Nation's Birds.* Whitlet Books, Stowmarket.

Mitchell, J., Placido, C., and Rose, R. 1974. Notes on a short-tailed Vole Plague at Eskdalemuir, Dumfries-shire. *The Transactions of the Dumfries-shire and Galloway Natural History and Antiquarian Society*, 3rd ser. Vol 11.

Murray, R.D., Holling, M., Dott, H.E.M. & Vandorne, P., 1998. *The Breeding Birds of South-east Scotland: a tetrad atlas 1988–1994.* SOC, Edinburgh.

Newton, I. 1984. Raptors in Britain – a review of the last 150 years. *BTO News* 131: 6–7.

Newton, I. 1994. Current Population levels in Diurnal Raptors in Britain. *The Raptor,* 1993–1994.

Noble, D. G., Raven, M. J. & Baillie, S.R. 2001. The Breeding Bird Survey 2000. *BTO Research Project 265.* BTO, Thetford.

Paton, R.E., Pike, O.G., 1929. *The Birds of Ayrshire.* H.F. & G. Witherby. London.

Pennington, M.G., Osborn, K., Harvey, P.V., Riddington, R., Okill, J.D., Ellis, P.M., and Heubeck, M. 2004. *The Birds of Shetland.* Christopher Helm, London.

Petty, S.J. 1999. Diet of Tawny Owls (*Strix aluco*) in Relation to Field Vole (*Microtus agrestis*) Abundance in a Conifer Forest in Northern England. Journal of Zoology, London 248, 451–465

Petty, S.J., Anderson, D.I.K., Davidson, M., Little, B., Sherrat, T.N., Thomas, C.J., Lambin, X. 2003. The decline of Common Kestrels *Falco tinnunculas* in a forested area of northern England : the role of predation by Northern Goshawks *Accipiter gentilis. Ibis* (2003), 145, 472-483.

Ratcliffe, D.A. 1980. *The Peregrine Falcon.* Poyser, Calton.

Rheinallt, T., Craik, J.C.A., Daw, P., Furness, R.W., Petty, S.J. & Wood, D. (Eds.) 2007. *Birds of Argyll.* Argyll Bird Club, Lochgilphead.

Riddle, G. 1986. *Kestrel on Arran.* Arran Naturalist 9: 4–12.

Riddle, G. 1992. *Seasons with the Kestrel.* Blandford, London.

Riddle, G.S. and Sheppard, G. 1999. Large Kestrel Clutch Sizes in South-West Scotland 1997–1998. *Scot. Birds* 20: 43.

Sharpe, Chris (Ed.) 2007. *Manx Bird Atlas*, Liverpool University Press.

St. John, C. 1919. *Wild Sports and Natural History of the Highlands*, p. 149. T. N. Foulis, London and Edinburgh.

Sharrock, J. T. R. 1976. *The Atlas of Breeding Birds in Britain and Ireland.* Poyser, Berkhamsted.

Shaw, G., & Riddle, G. 2003. Comparative responses of Barn Owls (*Tyto alba*) and Kestrel (*Falco tinnunculus*) to vole cycles in south-west Scotland. *Birds of Prey in a Changing Environment.* 7, 131–136. HMSO Ltd.

Shrubb, M. 2003. Farming and Birds: an Historical Perspective. *British Birds* 96: 158–177.

Shrubb, M. 1993. *The Kestrel.* Hamlyn, London.

Thom, V.M. 1986. *Birds in Scotland.* Poyser, Calton.

Village, A. 1986. Breeding performance of Kestrels at Eskdalemuir, south Scotland. *J. Zool., Lond.* (A) 2008: 367–378.

Village, A. 1990. *The Kestrel.* Poyser, London.